Murphy's Laws of Fishing
Murphy's Laws of Golf
The Official Rules of Bad Golf
The Complete French for Cats
A Dog's Night Before Christmas
A Cat's Night Before Christmas
French Cats Don't Get Fat
What's Worrying Gus?
X-Treme Latin
Latin for All Occasions
The Dick Cheney Code
Where's Saddam?
Skiing: A Snowslider's Dictionary
Fishing: An Angler's Dictionary
Golfing: A Duffer's Dictionary
Sailing: A Lubber's Dictionary
Computing: A Hacker's Dictionary
The Official Exceptions to the Rules of Golf
Bill Gates' Personal Super Secret Private Laptop
Zen for Cats
The Unshredded Files of Bill and Hillary Clinton
Bad Golf My Way
Poetry for Cats
The Way Things Really Work
The Official Politically Correct Dictionary and Handbook
The Pentagon Catalog
Bored of the Rings
Leslie Nielsen's Stupid Little Golf Book
Mulligan's Laws
The No Sweat Aptitude Test
Cooking: A Cook's Dictionary
Gardening: A Gardener's Dictionary
Miss Piggy's Guide to Life
Miss Piggy's Art Masterpieces

G⦿LF

AN UNOFFICIAL AND UNAUTHORIZED HISTORY OF THE WORLD'S MOST PREPOSTEROUS SPORT

A Parody

HENRY BEARD

Simon & Schuster

New York London Toronto Sydney

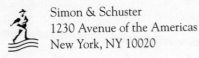

Simon & Schuster
1230 Avenue of the Americas
New York, NY 10020

Copyright © 2009 by Henry Beard

First Simon & Schuster hardcover edition December 2009

SIMON & SCHUSTER and colophon are registered
trademarks of Simon & Schuster, Inc.

For information about special discounts for bulk purchases,
please contact Simon & Schuster Special Sales at 1-866-506-1949
or business@simonandschuster.com.

The Simon & Schuster Speakers Bureau can bring authors to your
live event. For more information or to book an event contact the
Simon & Schuster Speakers Bureau at 1-866-248-3049 or visit our
website at www.simonspeakers.com.

Designed by Nancy Singer

Manuufactured in the United States of America

10 9 8 7 6 5 4 3 2 1

Library of Congress Cataloging-in-Publication data

Beard, Henry.
  Golf : an unofficial and unauthorized history of the world's most preposterous sport / Henry Beard.
        p. cm.
    1. Golf—History. I. Title.
  GV963.B43 2009
  796.352—dc22   2009019667
ISBN-13: 978-1-4391-6993-3 (alk. paper)
ISBN-10: 1-4391-6993-4 (alk. paper)

ACKNOWLEDGMENTS

The author gratefully acknowledges the invaluable assistance of the following distinguished experts in the field of golf historiography, without whose exhaustive studies and painstaking research this book would not have been able to achieve the very high standards of archival accuracy the subject demanded: Gordon Buncombe and Simon Balderdash of St. Andrews University; Sir Thomas Rot, Esq., of the Royal Golf Society; Brian Malarkey and Michael Baloney of Dublin College; Hendrik Hokum of the University of Delft; Jost Van Humbugger of the University of Antwerp; Hans Bosh and Kurt Bunk of Dusseldorf College; Pablo Folderol of the University of Valencia; Luigi Farrago of the University of Genoa; Michel Canard of the University of Versailles; Miss Martha Hooey of the Links Institute in Richmond, Virginia; Francis Crapola of San Ardo State College; Hiroshi Sayso of Kyoto University; Arpad Ersatz of the Hungarian Golf Association; and Vikram B.S. Bushwa of the University of Calcutta.

To

_____

(your name here)

a fine golfer and a keen student of the game whose
deep respect for the rich history of the sport is
clearly demonstrated by the presence in his or her
library of this truly remarkable book

CONTENTS

GOLF

INTRODUCTION

When I first set out to write a book tracing the origins and charting the evolution of this strange sport in which a number of special clubs are used to hit a small, stationary ball into a series of widely spaced holes in the ground, I encountered pretty much universal reactions of befuddlement and disbelief from my fellow players that could probably best be summarized as, "Who gives a rat's patootie about the history of golf? Just tell me how in hell to play the stupid game."

I was tempted to respond by quoting the famous admonition made by the great philosopher George Santayana (16-handicap, played a big fade, a demon with the flat stick)—namely, that those who do not study history are condemned to study much more difficult subjects like trigonometry, Latin, or Russian literature—but I realized they had a point.

After all, this frustrating, infuriating, but ultimately captivating pastime has plenty of far more pressing mysteries to unravel than the question of where it came from—truly knotty problems like taming a snaphook, or battling the yips, or curing a case of the shanks.

And, honestly, who cares whether the head case who dreamed the whole thing up was a Scottish whackjob, a Dutch whackjob, or even a Chinese whackjob? We still have to figure out how to slash a ball out of hip-high rough, or blast a sand shot from an unraked footprint in a bunker, or hit a duffed drive off the ladies' tee with dignity.

Well, the fact is that the numerous and often quite detailed accounts of the genesis and growth of golf really do have much of practical value to offer even casual students of the game, who can derive immediate and tangible benefits from little more than a passing familiarity with a few key items in the sport's rich chronology.

For instance, if your tee shot on a water hole lands in the drink, you might want to remind your fellow players of the royal decree promulgated by King James in 1606 guaranteeing "safe, free, and fair passage over all ye waters and washes of ye realm, be they firths, lochs, tarns, burns, runnels, sloughs, fens, or bogs, for all and sundry, and for their goods and chattels, without hindrance, fee, or penalty, from now and for all time."

Similarly, a golfer who finds his or her ball in an

obstructed lie behind a large tree would do well to recall Admiralty Order 27 issued by the Sea Lords of the Cinque Ports in 1557 reserving prime stands of timber for future use as spars in ships of the Royal Navy and requiring all persons to take such steps as are reasonably necessary to preserve particularly fine woodland specimens from harm, including, of course, preventing the damage that could be caused by a blocked shot that chipped the bark of an obvious candidate for conversion into the mast of a frigate.

And a competitor facing a hopeless downhill double-breaking twenty-five-foot money putt on the 18th hole of a Sunday skins match might choose to cite the Edinburgh Council's prohibition of 1592 against "playing golf in time of sermons" and insist on a draw, perhaps accompanying his opportune recollection of the ban on Sabbath play with a sharp slap to his forehead to display remorse at his prior forgetfulness of the obligation to engage in more appropriately pious pursuits on the day of rest.

Now surely, out of a sense of respect for the time-honored customs and centuries-old traditions of golf, and in recognition of the memorable exploits on the links of so many legendary players celebrated in its chronicles, you owe it to yourself and, yes, to the very spirit of this great game, to take a do-over on that tee shot that got wet, throw that stymied ball out into the fairway, and pick up that putt.

And in any event, always bear in mind that, as was so aptly remarked by the noted essayist and critic Ralph "Wild-o" Emerson (a scratch player but inclined to spray his drives, hence his nickname), the only reason it's called "golf" is that all the other four-letter words were already taken.

AUTHOR'S NOTE

All of the individual time line entries in the chronology contained in this book are based on actual facts or events recorded in contemporary accounts or reported by reputable sources. The various explications, amplifications, and digressions that follow the initial historical reference in each dated item basically consist of the very same thing most golfers encounter out on the course every day as the play this challenging game—a whole lot of really ridiculous lies.

I

TEEING OFF

732–1899

732

Relics of Saint Andrew, patron saint of Scotland and of golf, are brought from Constantinople to Cill Rim-hinn, the ancient Celtic site of the modern-day town of St. Andrews. The relics are said to include the apostle's right middle finger, a left kneecap with evidence of severe ACL damage, portions of a mangled rotator cuff, an ingenious hip-socket replacement made of ivory, a copper arthritis bracelet, and a pair of sandals with spikes on the soles.

733

In the first of a long series of miracles in Scotland attributed to Saint Andrew over the centuries, a dry well in Troon begins pumping pure whiskey and a flock of sheep in Carnoustie suddenly produce an abundance of a strange new wool that is a 50-50 blend of Polarfleece and polyester.

872

A contemporary account of various sports featured at the coronation of King Alfred the Great of the Saxons refers to players "driving balls wide over the fields." In addition to establishing the length of a solidly hit drive (220 yards) as his kingdom's basic unit of measurement (the furlong), the scholarly monarch presided over the standardization of the spelling and pronunciation of the key Anglo-Saxon four-letter words that are such an indispensable part of the game of golf.

1009

According to the noted golf historian Sir Walter Simpson, sometime early in the eleventh century a lone Scottish shepherd began idly hitting round pebbles with his shepherd's crook along the bare coastal links land where his flock grazed. One day, after watching his pebble disappear into a gorse bush, he dropped a new round pebble a couple of crook lengths away, rolled it over onto a nice tuft of turf, forgot the original stroke, ignored the lost-pebble penalty, hit a do-over shot, threw his pebble out of a sandy hollow, then gave himself a putt that was a full fifteen paces from the rabbit hole he was playing toward,

and thus, in a single afternoon, invented all the basic elements of modern golf except for product endorsements
and tiresome TV commentary.

1066

William the Conqueror defeats the Saxons at the Battle
of Hastings and establishes Norman rule over England,
bringing with him the rich repertoire of rude Gallic
hand gestures of disgust, contempt, and derision that
future golfers will find so effective when coupled with
English expletives.

1200–1250

Dongxuan Records maintained during the Song dynasty describe a game called *chuiwan* (rough translation:
"pointless and infuriating nonsense" or "source of earthly
discord") played with a set of ten clubs inlaid with jade
and gold (melamine and lead in the rental sets); balls
with pigskin covers and solid inner cores filled with beef,
pork, or shrimp; and a pair of delicate eight-foot-long
bamboo chopsticks for use as a ball retriever.

1297

Earliest recorded instance of a golflike game called *kolf* being played in Holland. The sport, which involved using a curved stick to hit a two-pound ball toward a goal post, was more challenging than it sounds since in addition to wearing wooden shoes, the *kolfers* wore a wooden glove and, depending on the weather, either wooden shorts or wooden foul-weather gear. *Kolf* is variously translated as "stick," "club," "bat," "chunk," "skull," "choke," and "cheat."

1320

The Declaration of Arbroath formally recognizes Scotland's conversion to Christianity by Saint Andrew. The parallel Declaration of Areyoudaft? specifically rejects Islam due to its prohibition against beers at the halfway house and rounds of cocktails in the taproom; Judaism for its dietary laws forbidding the consumption of hot dogs and of bacon, a key ingredient of club sandwiches; and Buddhism because of its nonviolent principles that seem to preclude deliberately hitting balls into a slower group of players on the hole ahead.

1353

The first printed reference to the game of *chole*, a team sport popular in Flanders played with iron-headed clubs and wooden balls that was a sort of cross-country version of a modern-day charity golf scramble with some croquet thrown in. *Chole* no doubt had an influence on golf, but there was one major difference between the two games: *Choleurs* were actually permitted to hit their opponents' balls away from the target or into a hazard from time to time, instead of just stepping on them, running them over with a golf cart, or surreptitiously kicking them into a ditch.

1421

Scottish soldiers sent to help a French garrison town resist an English siege are introduced to *chole*. On their return home, the Scots officers are thought to have brought back key elements of the French game, which were soon incorporated into the native version. They also imported several other useful pieces of French sporting culture that have become inseparable parts of golf: *le boîtement truqe* (the fake limp), *la tape sur les nerfs* (the needle), *la toux opportune* (the well-timed cough), *l'éternuement étouffe* (the stifled sneeze), and *la feinte du lâchement d'un pet faite avec lèvre et langue* (the simulated farting sound made with the lips and tongue).

1425-1435

A Ming dynasty silkscreen scroll clearly depicts Emperor Xuande tapping a ball toward a golf hole on what appears to be a formal putting green. Recent excavations of Ming tombs have turned up fascinating artifacts that seem to support the case for this Chinese version of the game, including a teak sedan chair designed to be carried by four coolies with a space in back to strap on two golf bags, a tray for balls, and a pair of cup holders; a set of exquisitely detailed, life sized, terra-cotta statuettes depicting the Ten Auspicious Positions of the Heavenly Swing; and the graves of more than a hundred ritually executed caddies.

1457

Concerned that these sports are taking valuable time away from archery practice during a period of military threats from the English, King James II of Scotland issues a decree that "the futballe and golfe be utterly cryed down and not to be used," but the order specifically exempts "the hoolieganisme and the wilde rowdinesse of the futballe fannes" as well as "the hurlinge of the clubbes as be practised upon the linkes."

1470

The ban on golf is renewed by James III, and several new sports are added to the list: "the puffe-poole, the pynge-ponge, the slappe-jacques, the knocke-hockie, and the tossinge of the frissbie."

1491

The golf ban is reaffirmed by James IV with language expressly proscribing what appear to have been attempts to continue playing the game under different names, including "flogge, goofe, golaff, screweballe, and feck-heade."

1492

Columbus discovers the future birthplace of Tiger Woods.

1502

With the signing of the Treaty of Glasgow, hostilities between England and Scotland come to an end, and the ban on golf is lifted. A clause in the treaty insisted upon by the Scots explicitly permits the wearing of kilts while playing golf, thereby setting the stage for centuries of tasteless and laughable golfing attire.

1502–1504

James IV makes the first recorded purchases of sets of golf clubs and balls, as noted in the accounts of the Lord High Treasurer in two separate entries about a year and a half apart:

> "Item: The xxi day of September, to the bowmaker of Perth for clubs and clubbhead covvers bearing the likenesses of a Lyone, an Unicorne, a Griffin, a Falcone, Punch, Judie, Tobey, a Crockodyle, and the Deville—xiii shillings."

> "Item: The third day of Februar, to the King to play at the Golf with the Earl of Bothwell, for Golf Clubbis and Ballis to the King that he playit with, and for severall Devises to aide the swinge, these being a sort of Strappe to binde the elbowe, a Sticke to estoppe the hip swaye, and an Helmet to fixe the head in playce duringe the takinge of the stroke. Also a douzaine of burstinge Ballis made of chalke for purposes of tomfoolerie—xlii, lx shillings."

1513

In a letter to Cardinal Wolsey, Catherine of Aragon, Queen Consort of England and first wife of Henry VIII, writes that "all the king's subjects be very glad, Master Almaner, I thank God, to busy with the golf, for they take it for pastime." The queen's pleasure at the rapid spread of the game in the wake of the peace treaty is tempered, however, by concerns for the players' health. "I am nonetheless troubled to observe," her letter continues, "that the golfers in their play are oft convulsed with coughing and sneezing fits, as if they had the catarrh, and as well are wont to limp most lamentably, and tho' it perhaps be indelicate of me to make mention of it, are sore afflicted by flatulence." She finishes the missive with an interesting ecclesiastical inquiry: "Pray tell me if rumors of a recent miracle ascribed to holy St. Andrew are worthy of credence, namely that a stream in the environs of Muirfield for a fortnight flowed not with that aqueous liquid that the trouts are accustomed to encounter in their fishy pursuits, but rather with undiluted beer."

1527

The earliest printed reference to someone other than a king, earl, or duke playing golf is published in a local chronicle that describes Sir Robert Maule of Carnoustie as "a man of comely behaviour, of high stature, sanguine in colour both of skin and hair, choleric of nature and subject to sudden anger. He had great delight in hawking and hunting. Likewise he exercised the golf, and ofttimes passed to Barry Links when the wager was for drink and he would playact the duffer at the practise before the match and counterfeit poor form and a hacking style of swing and beg of mercy that his adversary would vouchesafe him four strokes a side and then would suddenly find his game and bestow on the hapless sod such a clobbering as would have him think to had been waylaid by a highwayman and coldcocked from behind and rudely dealt a mighty blow to the back of his head with a bag of sand."

1530

Completion of the set of detailed miniature paintings in *The Book of Hours*, an illuminated manuscript depicting life in sixteenth-century Flanders. Marginal illustrations on several pages seem to clearly show golfers with clubs and balls, including a player accidentally hitting another player on the head while making warm-up swings, a duffer standing in a classic follow-through position with the ball still sitting on the ground between his feet, another breaking a club over his knee, a third relieving himself behind a tree, an exasperated golfer throwing a club into a pond, and a sly competitor dropping a ball while another player's back is turned.

1553

John Hamilton, Archbishop of St. Andrews, formally endorses the townspeople's traditional privilege of free access over the adjacent links land with a decree that confirms the "right and possession, property and community of the said links in playing at golf without any impediment to be made to them in any time coming." In a remarkable display of foresight, he also guarantees to all future citizens of St. Andrews "the sole right to offer for sale at a good price beer mugs and towels and hats and divers and sundry knickknacks and trinkets showing the great Seal of the Town of Saint Andrews and signs and tokens of the Saint Himself and place mats and trays and platters with scenery of the links and to make inns of their dwellings and offer a bed and a breakfast to such travelers as may journey hence from far and wide to play at golf on said links and for that favor to levy a charge of an arm and a leg."

1567

The first known reference to a lady golfer is contained in one of the charges brought against Mary Queen of Scots in the trial for treason that led to her execution. According to the accusation, just a few days after the murder of her husband, Lord Darnley, she had been seen "playing golf in the fields beside Seton" and further, that she "played in so dilatory a fashion, all the while prattling and gossiping with her ladies-in-waiting, and redisposing her costume and fussing with her tresses, and making innumerable rehearsal swings and fidgets with the club and shiftings of her stance, and refusing to quit play upon a hole notwithstanding that the putt she surveyed constituted her twenty-fourth stroke thereon, and thus in every aspect of her play upon the course did present a grave and mortal menace to the game of golf."

1570

A noteworthy grudge match between the brutal and law-less Earl of Cassillis and the Abbot of Crossragruel takes place on the links at Ayr. The reputed wager is said to be for the monk's nose. The competition is the first-known skins game and is the likely source of the terms "no blood" and "no skin off my nose." It probably also inaugurated the custom of awarding extra points for "specs," like greenies, sandies, barkies, and splashies, although at Ayr the bonus would have been given for screamies (getting closest to the hole while being tortured), handies (getting up and down while wearing manacles), sparkies (saving par while dodging flaming arrows), and gashies (sinking a birdie putt while being stabbed).

1588

The failure of the invasion of England and Scotland by the Spanish Armada sets back golf in Spain for the four hundred years it will take to produce—and for the world to prepare for—Seve Ballesteros.

1592

The town council of Edinburgh issues a proclamation against playing golf on Sundays "in time of sermons." It is important to note, however, that what appears to be a sweeping prohibition is in reality a much more limited ban—the statute applies only to the specific period when actual preaching is taking place. This fact helps explain the considerable popularity of a trio of Scots clergymen of the time, including Jack Robinson, the Fast Pastor of Aberdeen, who could recite the entire Sermon on the Mount in five seconds flat; the Rev. Seth Pithy, the Brief Preacher of Dundee, who was widely acclaimed for his succinct "hundred-words-of-God-or-less" sermons; and Gordon Dawdle, the Tardy Parson of Fife, who never set foot in the pulpit until well after sundown.

1618

James VI and I issues a proclamation supporting the right of the people to play golf on Sundays. An avid player, the dual monarch of Scotland and England made yet another crucial if inadvertent contribution to the game occasioned by the strain of remembering that he was both James VI (the Sixth) of Scotland and James I (the First) of England. This computational confusion caused him from time to time to enter a III on his score-card instead of, say, an VIII, or a V instead of an X. The delicate problem of disputing the royal score led to the game's speedy adoption of Arabic numerals.

1620

Approximate date of the introduction of the "feathery" ball, a small round pouch of stitched bull's-hide leather stuffed with feathers that quickly displaces the widely used wooden golf ball. In an early demonstration of the ceaseless search for a technological edge that will long be the hallmark of a fiercely competitive industry, several ball makers almost immediately introduce brands with dubious special performance features, including the Windrider, containing seagull feathers ("to sail far above the waters"); the Whizzer, loaded with a blend of partridge, quail, and grouse feathers ("ready to explode from the heather, whins, and underbrush like a flushed game bird"); the Buzzard, with a stuffing of turkey vulture feathers ("to make carrion of the competition"); and the Wise Birdie, filled with parrot feathers ("the ball you can talk to"). The canny manufacturers also offered

a pair of unsportsmanlike dud balls with deliberately degraded flight characteristics intended for surreptitious substitution during a match—the Thrice-Cursed Ball of Ill Omen and Doom, crammed with a mixture of albatross, raven, and owl feathers, and the Flightless Wonder, packed with feathers from a dodo.

1630

Sir Robert Gordon heaps praise on the links at Dornoch, claiming that "they doe surpass the fields of St. Andrews." This is not only the first comparative course rating but also the last time that every golf course in the world—Ayr, Barry, Cullen, Dornoch, Leith, Montrose, Musselburgh, North Inch, Stirling, and St. Andrews—will make the top-ten list.

1641

Charles I is playing a golf match at Leith when he gets word of the outbreak of the Irish Rebellion that began the Civil War. The revolt of Catholic Ireland was triggered by a false rumor that the English king planned to abolish the mulligan and the gimme. These two fundamental indulgences had been officially sanctioned by Pope Pius V in the papal bull *De Ictu Iterato et Conces-*

sionibus but equally explicitly condemned by the fiery Scots evangelist John Knox, whose widely circulated (though very sparsely attended) two-and-a-half-hour sermon "Sinful Golfers in the Handes of an Angry God" proclaimed that "there be no do-overs in Hell, and ye shall yip the knee knockers back and forth about the cup for all Eternity." Incidentally, there are two versions of history detailing the king's reaction to the report of the uprising: On receiving the news Charles either hurried away to prepare for war or coolly finished the match before setting off. Needless to say, which account is correct depends on whether he was winning at the time.

1642

The town of Aberdeen licenses John Dickson as a ball maker. A gifted innovator, Dickson experiments with various designs for golf ball packages, including an awkward billiards-style six-ball triangular rack, an inconvenient circular five-ball tin, and a bulky four-ball cube, before settling on the simple, portable three-ball sleeve that fast becomes the industry standard. He also develops a cheap, durable range ball with a goatskin cover stuffed with pigeon feathers treated with a malodorous mixture of guano and fish oil to discourage theft.

1646

While a prisoner of the Scots, Charles I plays golf in the fields outside Newcastle. A wildly errant driver of the ball, the captive king originates a much-used golf expression when, after failing to hit his ball out from behind a tree, he remarks, "I am as much in jail out upon the course as I am in yon castle."

1649

Execution of Charles I. Even on the scaffold, the doomed monarch displays his uncanny gift for coining golfing terms, grumbling to the assembled spectators that Oliver Cromwell has settled the "contest of wills and match of wits betwixt we two contenders for Supremacy in a manner most unsporting—by my sudden Death."

1650

Charles II plays golf during his brief time as King in Scotland. Closely supervised by dour Scottish ministers who disapprove of any strong language or the taking of the Lord's name in vain, the young sovereign shows he has inherited his father's way with words (as well as his nasty slice) when, desperate to find an acceptable way to express his profound dismay at wayward tee shots, he invents pig Latin.

1658

The first mention of a truly public links is contained in a petition by Thomas Harbottle, of Vincent Square, who sends a letter of complaint to the governors of the adjacent college that owned the golfing fields referring to certain "parties who do sleep in their carriages over the Night that they may be first upon the links at Dawn, and do disturb the slumbers of the local habitants with disputes as to the Rights of Priority of Play, which they make at the top of their Lungs at first Lighte of Day."

1672

The account books of John Foulis, a golfer in Ravel-stoun, contain an entry with the first known three-digit golf club bar bill.

1682

The first international golf match, between England and Scotland, takes place at Leith Links in Edinburgh. The English side is represented by two noblemen in the Scottish court; the Scottish side consists of the Duke of York (later King James II) and a commoner, John Pater-sone, a poor shoemaker who is the first in a long line of "fluky" low-scoring ringers who will become the main-stay of member-guest tournaments in centuries to come. The match, which was handily won by Scotland, also featured the earliest display of boorish Ryder Cup–style behavior by chauvinistic crowds who booed the other nation's competitors, cheered their missed putts, and traded nativist insults, like the Scots' taunts of "Kiss my thistle" and "Bite my haggis," and the English gibes of "Up your loch" and "Stick it in your firth." The match was notable as well for the first recorded appearance of a caddie, the Duke of York's attendant, Andrew Dick-son, who set the tone for the conduct of future professional loopers when, on the fifth tee of the final round, he seized the sketch pad of a local artist who he claimed had interrupted the duke's backswing with the scratching of his pencil, and threw it and the offending portraitist into a drainage ditch.

1687

Thomas Kincaid publishes *Thoughts on Golve*, the first book with extensive references to how golf clubs are made. The Venerable and Diligent Guild of Club Makers quickly secures an order from the Lords of Session banning Kincaid's work on the grounds that several of his chapters betray their proprietary trade secrets, including "The Use of Varnish to Mask Imperfections," "Imparting the Hidden Flaw That Will Oblige a Costly Repair," "How Mere Tinkering Can Be Made to Mimic Innovation," "The Appeal of a Novel Design to the Duffer's Vanity," "The Virtues of Offering for Sale a Bewildering Multiplicity of Implements," and "Making the Case for the Unsuitability of Secondhand Sticks."

1721

Earliest mention of golf at Glasgow Green, the first course in the relatively desolate west of Scotland. The Glasgow city fathers attempted to encourage the new links with the oldest known municipal advertising campaign to encourage tourism to a golfing destination, but their typically self-deprecatory slogan—"Glasga', it's nae half as bad as ye may think"—fails to transform the Clydeside region into the Myrtle Beach of Scotland.

1724

First newspaper report of a game of golf, a match at Leith Links between Alexander Elphinstone and Captain John Porteous. The press account recorded a number of additional "firsts," among them the first misspelling of a player's name, the first incorrect listing of the final posted scores, the first erroneous statement of the amount of the wager, the first misquote of a participant's remarks, the first wildly inflated estimate of the size of the crowd, the first missing paragraph containing a description of the key moments in the match, and the first misinformed opinion about the significance of the outcome made by a member of the editorial staff who was not present at the competition and was totally unfamiliar with the game.

1743

Publication of Thomas Mathison's mock-epic poem, *The Goff*. In rhyming couplets, Mathison describes most of the notable golfers of the age and provides some useful insights into the state of the game at that time. In a pair of verses toward the end of the poem he also makes a quite remarkable prediction, noting that whereas his aim has been "to celebrate the play of golfdom's greats, their styles, their skills, and all their winning traits," perhaps in years to come "some future bard may take a different tack, and tell of doings in the Caddyshack."

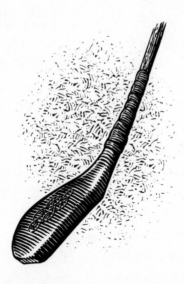

1744

The first open golf competition takes place in Edinburgh after golfers at Leith Links petition the city fathers to provide a silver club as a trophy. After making a series of counteroffers of a silver toothpick, a silver ball marker, and a silver shoehorn, the penny-pinching magistrates finally relent and provide the prize. The first winner is local surgeon John Rattray, whose victory is somewhat tarnished by later revelations that in his haste to leave his dispensary and repair to the links for the tournament, he had ordered an enema for someone suffering from an earache and had removed the tonsils of a patient with a broken leg.

1754

The first Rules of Golf are codified by the St. Andrews Golfers. The thirteen "Conditions and Regulations" governing play contain the basic principles of the game, like the stipulation that the ball be played as it lies, the provisions for the assessment of penalties for lost balls and for drops taken from hazards, and the requirement that the player farthest from the hole hit first. The Golfers also promulgated a separate list of twenty-two "Exemptions and Concessions" from the Rules of Golf, including the long-established Mulligan on the first tee and Gimmes both for putts shorter than the distance from the bottom of the putter grip to the top of the head of the putter and for any fourth putt, regardless of its length; the Freebie, which allowed for play without penalty of a different, but similar, ball, chanced upon during an unsuccessful search conducted in reasonable proximity to the point where the original ball was lost; the Wee Bit Thithery, which permitted a golfer to play a ball, without penalty, that was just a little out of bounds; and Winter Rules, which authorized players to roll their balls over onto preferred lies at any time during the twelve-month period that comprised the Scottish winter.

1759

First mention of stroke play, as opposed to match play, at St. Andrews. First round of golf that takes more than three hours to complete.

1764

The first four holes at St. Andrews are combined into two, reducing the standard round from 22 holes to 18. From now on, players in danger of losing high-stakes matches will fake the symptoms of a heart attack on the 9th hole instead of the 11th; it will begin raining steadily on the 12th hole instead of the 16th; the clubhouse bar where golfers go after a round to drown their sorrows and welsh on their bets will be known as the 19th hole, not the 23rd; and married golfers with nonplaying wives who would previously have had to concoct a preposterous tale of alien abduction to account for a two-round, 44-hole, all-day blowout will now be able to explain away an episode of extended 36-hole play with a simple lie about a flat tire.

Formation of the first golf club, the Honourable Company of Edinburgh Golfers. Establishment of the first committees. First debate about status of junior members. First discussion of playing privileges of spouses "and others of significance." First five changes in policy covering guest play.

1766

Formation of the Blackheath Golf Club in London, the first golf club outside of Scotland. This earliest English golfing society was noted for a legendary foursome of deeply incompetent players whose names and faults have been immortalized in golfing lore: Albert Shank, the 4th Earl of Hosel; Rev. Quentin Whiff; Sir Francis Dunch; and Thomas Snaphook, Esq.

A group of St. Andrews golfers agrees to dine together every other week at a local tavern with each "to pay a shilling for his dinner, the absent as well as the present," thereby establishing the first of many irritating club fees, the monthly meal minimum.

1767

During the annual Silver Club competition, James Durham turns in a score of 94 at St. Andrews, setting a course record that will stand for eighty-six years. Considering the fact that a top player who barely broke 100 had the low round in a major championship, it is almost certain that the lifelong ambition of a decent amateur golfer of this era was to shoot his weight, not his age.

1768

Construction of the Golf House at Leith, the first club-house. First recriminations over wildly underestimated construction costs. First assessments. First inexplicable disappearance of a set of club account books.

1774

Thomas McMillan provides a silver cup for a competition among the Musselburgh golfers, which he proceeds to win. Overcome by relief at his success in reclaiming the costly utensil that he had impulsively donated in a moment of alcohol-fueled generosity, McMillan celebrated his victory by giving the cup a heartfelt smooch, thereby establishing the tradition of golf tournament winners planting a kiss on the trophy at postround awards ceremonies. The chastened McMillan retired the silver cup on the spot, replacing it in all future competitions with the more modest prize of a silver thimble.

1779

Golf is played for the first time in America, by Scottish officers quartered in New York during the Revolutionary War. The inhabitants of the city display little interest in the new game, but they do exhibit the sharp eye for a sucker for which they are justly famed as they sell the gullible redcoats worthless time-shares in a nonexistent beachfront golf resort in the balmy, palm-studded, sand-fringed, sun-kissed paradise of Coney Island.

1786

Formation of the South Carolina Golf Club in Charleston, the earliest known instance of golf being played by Americans. The Carolina club is also celebrated as the site of the first four-hour round, the first beer served from a vehicle circulating around the course (a horse-drawn wagon), and the first telling of the joke with the punch line, "hit, drag Harry."

1788

The Edinburgh Golfers adopt a dress code requiring their members to wear a club uniform of a red jacket during their play, thereby inaugurating an ongoing sartorial catastrophe that will result two centuries hence in the inevitable appearance on golf courses of players sporting a pair of green golf pants matched with a pink polo shirt.

1806

The golfers of St. Andrews decide to make the Captaincy of the Club an elective office. First disputed election of a captain. First disputed club election decided by a coin toss. First disputed coin toss.

1810

First ladies' golf competition held at Musselburgh, a noted fishing port. The majority of the female players are in fact commercial fisherwomen who bequeath to the club, and all golfing posterity, a pair of handy gadgets they employed to ready their rusty swings for play: a practice net whose ball-stopping mesh smelled vaguely of haddock and a weighted warm-up club adapted from the cudgels used to stun unruly cod.

1826

First record of the importation from America of hickory, a tough, supple wood ideal for golf shafts. Supplies of premium wood declined and prices rose throughout the nineteenth century, and a careful inspection of golf clubs surviving from the era shows that about a third of them were actually made from a wide array of inferior substitutes stained to look like the real thing, including elm, ash, birch, locust, dogwood, hazelnut, sassafras, pussy willow, swamp maple, kumquat, and ginkgo.

1829

The first circular metal holecutter is fabricated at Musselburgh Links. It produced a cup diameter of 4¼ inches, which becomes, by default, the standard dimension of a golf hole. Some physicists believe that the persistence of this obviously insufficient width for the putting target is proof that no technologically advanced future generation of golf-playing humans will develop a workable time machine that would make possible a return to the past to rectify this intolerable situation. Other theorists argue, however, that it is equally possible that the hole was once, say, 3¼ inches in diameter, and time travelers did in fact pay a visit to nineteenth-century Scotland to rewrite this critical specification but had a seriously warped idea of what constituted reasonable proportions for the hole. Adding credence to this thought-provoking thesis is the striking fact that all at once, at almost exactly the same time, separate teeing areas start being set up on ground adjacent to the previous green rather than right on it; practically simultaneously and seemingly out of nowhere, ball washers suddenly appear; and at virtually the identical moment, the first beer bottle with a cap that can be removed with a simple metal opener is abruptly introduced.

1832

A mechanical grass-cutting device for trimming the turf on golf links is perfected. The introduction of the new mowers puts an end to more than two centuries of fruitless efforts to develop a breed of sheep that will graze the fairways in the distinctive crisscross diamond pattern that is the wet dream of all club members and the nightmare of every greenkeeper.

1833

The Perth Golfing Society is granted the designation "Royal" by William IV, becoming the first club to receive this distinction. It is not the last. In years to come, more than seventy golfing locales get the regal nod, including three miniature golf courses (Royal Lilliputt in Liverpool, Royal Dinkylinks in Bournemouth, and Royal Cubbyholes in Swansea); a pair of pitch-and-putts (Royal Parthreestie in Glasgow and Royal Feathershot in Bristol); and one practice facility (Royal Chelsea Pier, an indoor driving range on the boardwalk in the famed seaside resort town of Blackpool).

Thanks to spirited lobbying by Sir Hugh Lyon Playfair, a highly respected (and aptly named) member of the St. Andrews Golfers, the stymie rule, which had always required players to putt around a ball blocking the path to the cup, is temporarily suspended. The rule is reinstated the following year after strenuous counterpressure is exerted on the St. Andrews governing board by Playfair's longtime nemesis, the archtraditionalist Gordon Shitforbrains.

1834

Miffed by the prior selection of Perth as the first recipient of a royal designation, the St. Andrews Golfers petition the palace for a similar recognition. William IV obliges, awarding the club the honorific it now bears, "Royal and Ancient Golf Club of St. Andrews," a pared-down version of the title the St. Andrews players had originally requested: "Royal, Ancient, Glorious, Marvelous, Splendid, Magnificent, Transcendent, Triumphant, Incomparable, Phenomenal, Fabulous, Awesome, Superlative, and Stupendous."

1836

Samuel Messieux hits the longest drive ever recorded with a feathery ball, an astounding 361-yard smash. The legitimacy of the feat is later called into question when a close examination of the ball shows that it is a smaller-than-regulation "bandit ball" with a horsehide cover made from a recently deceased thoroughbred and a filling of tail feathers from fighting cocks "juiced up" with a handful of watch springs.

1848

Introduction of the gutta-percha golf ball, a cheap, lively, and practically indestructible ball made from an easily molded brownish red resinous latex gum extracted from Malayan rubber trees. In a stroke of luck that helped preserve golf's reputation as a genteel game, three quite similar substances from related tropical plants—kutta-farta, shitta-brikka, and fukka-ducka—prove totally unsuitable for use in the manufacture of golf balls.

1857

Publication of H. B. Farnie's *The Golfer's Manual: Being an Historical and Descriptive Account of the National Game of Scotland* (under the pseudonym A Keen Hand), the earliest known golf instruction book. Since it is the first text ever written purporting to teach the game, it is also the only golf instruction manual that does not directly contradict key swing tips and pieces of playing advice in previous manuals, or steal large sections from them, or dismiss them as worthless.

1858

Allan Robertson, the first great professional golfer, shoots a 79 at St. Andrews, thus becoming the first golfer ever to break 80 at the storied links. During the legendary round, he also originates the complete repertory of facial expressions and hand gestures that modern-day pros still use to convey disbelief at missed putts: the head-back, eyes-to-the-sky look of shock and disbelief at a lip-out; the putter lightly tossed upward, then deftly caught after the ball burns the edge of the cup; the disgusted sweep-away of nonexistent debris from the line of a putt that rocketed six feet past the hole; and the nonchalant, back-of-the-putter-blade, pissed-off tap-in of a ball that came to rest on the very edge of the hole.

1861

Old Tom Morris, the lifelong partner and one-time student of Allan Robertson, wins the first British Open at Prestwick. Emulating his mentor's gift for useful golfing gestures, the normally reserved Scot marks his victory on the 18th green with the first-known fist pump, and the first celebratory knuckle tap with his caddie. The local newspaper grumbles disapprovingly that "he behaved as if he had scored a knockout in a boxing match," but it manages to maintain golfing journalism's traditional standards of reporting accuracy by spelling his name

"Morse" and erroneously listing the winning score as "2 to 1 in overtime" rather than 176.

1864

Old Tom Morris is appointed Keeper of the Greens at St. Andrews. Although this position is the precursor of the modern job of course superintendent, in Morris's time it comprised all of the functions now undertaken by several club employees, and Old Tom in effect wore three hats: As the greenkeeper, he was charged with the upkeep of the course; as the golf professional, he supervised instruction and ran the pro shop; and as the caddie master, he rode herd on the caddies, some of whom were in effect junior or assistant professionals. The burden of all these duties was considerable, but Morris, a sly Caledonian if there ever was one, contrived an ingenious stratagem for handling the pressures. Basically faking what nowadays would be interpreted as the symptoms of a severe multiple-personality disorder, Morris actually *did* wear three separate hats—a flat tweed cap as greenkeeper, a tam-o'-shanter as professional, and a glengarry bonnet as caddie master—and he spoke in a different tone of voice for each role: a raspy croak, a lilting burr, or a high-pitched cackle. Depending on whatever was the nature of the complaint, request, or suggestion made by any given member, he would adopt the persona of whichever of the triad of Morrises clearly was not responsible for handling the particular matter—for example, the greenkeeper, if, say, the head had flown off the end of a recently purchased club, or the caddie master if one of the greens was suddenly overrun with nettles. In extreme cases, he would don a Viking-style horned helmet and "channel" the spirit of Morragh, the mythical Wild Mon of the Moors, and begin chanting in ancient Celtic, an intimidating performance that was greatly enhanced by his ability to foam at the mouth at will.

1867

Formation at St. Andrews of the first Ladies' Golf Club. Responding to a request from this new society, the Royal and Ancient Golf Club initially proposes to give female players exclusive use of the links on the thirteenth day of any month that happens to fall on a Friday; on any day during a month on which there occurs a second full moon, or "blue moon"; and on February 29 of every leap year. When this openhanded offer is deemed insufficient, the governors grudgingly give in to the inevitable and agree to set aside one day a week for the women, thus establishing the now-universal tradition of Tuesday as Ladies' Day. Unbeknownst to the ladies, however, the club bigwigs give Tuesday an additional hidden designation as Labor Day and instruct the greenkeeping staff to restrict to that day any major course-disrupting work, including resodding the bunkers, aerating the greens, weeding the tee boxes, setting brushfires in the gorse, shooting the rabbits, and poisoning the crows.

1868

Young Tom Morris wins the first of four consecutive Open championships, a feat as yet unequaled. Old Tom's talented son demonstrates that he has a genius for marketing as well as golfing when he shows up for the tournament with clothing and equipment promoting various products and services he has endorsed for a hefty fee, including a Wedgwood logo on his cap, advertisements for Earl Grey Tea and Bovril Beef Extract on his jacket, and a Burberry golf bag.

1875

Following the untimely death of his wife in childbirth, Young Tom Morris dies of a broken heart. Equally broken-hearted are the despondent manufacturers of Highlands Pride Traditional Scots Shortbread who have to dispose of six thousand packages of their tasty product that feature a picture of Young Tom and the unfortunate slogan, "I couldna' live without this bonny, bonny biscuit!"

Founding of the Oxford University and Cambridge University Golf Clubs. First debate on a golf rule. The topic under discussion: "Resolved: That there being no tiny Rakes lying in or around the Divot Holes in the Fairway, these Scrapes and Hollows are not Pocket Hazards or Runt Bunkers, and it should thus be permissible to remove a Ball therefrom without Penalty."

1876

Birth of Bernard Darwin, grandson of Charles Darwin and one of the greatest golf writers of all time. Perhaps reflecting the familial genetic influence that his illustrious forebear first identified, his writings often explore similar Darwinian themes, including *Natural Club Selection*, which traces the evolution of golfing equipment from the primitive thick bludgeons with spikes sticking out of them that were used mainly to hit other players to the more specialized lightweight sticks, staves, and staffs that were employed primarily, though not exclusively, to hit the ball; *Swing Like a Monkey*, which emphasizes a very long "reach for the banana" takeaway move; *The Origin of Slices*, which attributes this most common of errant golf shots to the development of the opposable thumb; and *The Descent of the Henchman*, which propounds the somewhat offbeat theory that, based on their drinking habits, caddies are descended from fish.

1878

During the second of his three consecutive victories in the British Open, Jamie Anderson scores the first ace ever recorded in a championship on the 17th hole at Prestwick. It's a noteworthy achievement, but even more remarkable is the foresight of the members of the Prestwick Golf Club who procured hole-in-one insurance from Lloyd's of London and thus do not have to foot the bill for the purchase price of Anderson's prize—a sporty two-seat pony cart with flame-pattern side panels and a spoiler.

1880

Ball makers, who had previously used tack hammers to painstakingly pockmark the outsides of gutta-percha balls by hand with a custom-made matrix of aerodynamically beneficial indentations, now begin to employ pressure molds to quickly imprint a regular pattern of tiny hollows onto the ball covers. Although the new dimpled balls clearly display enhanced flight characteristics,

their chief advantage—and the main reason for their instant popularity—was their uniform appearance, which greatly simplified a stealthy, penalty-free drop through a hole in the pocket and down the pants leg of a nearly identical replacement for a lost ball.

1884

Formation of the Oakhurst Golf Club at White Sulphur Springs, West Virginia. A small portion of the historic layout survives as the first hole of the noted modern course, the Homestead. The tee of this hole has the further distinction of having once been the site of both the deepest reported rage-provoked club stab, a tremendous earth-piercing tomahawk blow with a driving iron that embedded its thin metal head a full 11¾ inches below the surface of the turf, and the longest throw of a golf club, a prodigious 114-foot heave that set a record that stood until the introduction of the long putter more than a hundred years later.

1886

Ignoring credible threats of assassination by Republican zealots, the Irish Secretary, Arthur Balfour, later Prime Minister, plays golf at Phoenix Park in Dublin, thereby achieving the distinction of being the only known golfing visitor to Ireland who was actually more likely to be killed on an Irish golf course than on a road driving to or from it.

1888

Founding of the Saint Andrew's Golf Club in Yonkers, the first club in the New York metropolitan area. First golf match settled in a lawsuit in federal court. First subpoena of a scorecard. First indictment of a caddy.

1889

Old Tom Morris is hired to lay out the Royal County Down links course in Newcastle, Ireland, "for a sum not to exceed four pounds." Setting a precedent that will be followed by course designers in the decades to come, Morris goes way over budget, and the final price tag for the design job soars to a whopping five pounds, six shillings, and twopence. The club members begrudge the overrun but finally relent and cough up the inflated fee when the canny Scot proposes to cut costs and meet the original figure by converting the layout to a pitch-and-putt and changing club's name to Royal County Up-and-Down.

1890

The word "bogey" is introduced. Confusingly, its original meaning was not "1 over par," but actually something much closer to "par"—the score a first-rate player playing excellent, but not necessarily perfect, golf would be likely to achieve on any given course. As equipment and players alike rapidly improved, golfers started to regularly take a full stroke less to play many of the holes, and "bogey" soon acquired its current meaning. Nevertheless, a general sense of vagueness still seems to hang over the whole thing, which may help explain why modern-day golfers who record a score of 1, 2, 3, or even 4 over par will from time to time unwittingly report that they had a bogey.

1891

Shinnecock Hills Golf Club, the site of four future U.S. Open tournaments, is founded in Southampton, on Long Island. Although it has the appearance and much of the spirit of a traditional Scottish seaside links, it nonetheless possesses a thoroughly American pedigree since it is located on a piece of land allegedly stolen from Indians whose tribal name it also appropriated.

1893

Founding of the Chicago Golf Club. First gimme putt conceded at gunpoint. First armed course marshal. First tournament with both a shotgun start and a shotgun finish.

1894

Formation of the United States Golf Association by five private golf clubs in the Northeast and Midwest. As its first official act, the new organization stipulates the size (0.68" diameter) and weight (0.62 ounce) of the regulation blackball to be used in club membership elections to exclude minorities and persons belonging to undesirable ethnic groups.

Beginning of a remarkable two decades of dominance of championship golf by "the Great Triumvirate" of J. H. Taylor, Harry Vardon, and James Braid, a threesome of talented contemporaries who among them won the British Open sixteen times in the next twenty-one years. On only four other occasions during the coming century will trios of such preeminent players appear together simultaneously on the golfing scene: Walter Hagen, Gene Sarazen, and Bobby Jones in the 1920s; Byron Nelson, Ben Hogan, and Sam Snead in the 1940s and 1950s; Arnold Palmer, Jack Nicklaus, and Gary Player in the 1960s; and in the period from 1995 to 2010, Tiger Woods, Tiger Woods, and Tiger Woods.

1895

In its first major ruling on noncomplying clubs, the USGA bans the use of pool cues as putters. It is a testament to the ingenuity and resourcefulness of the newly minted American golfer that the sport's regulating body soon finds it necessary to specifically outlaw a number of other pieces of nonconforming equipment, including croquet mallets, hockey sticks, fungo bats, slingshots, jai alai scoops, handheld spring-loaded clay pigeon launchers, and catapults.

Opening of the first public course in the United States, at Van Cortlandt Park in the Bronx. The game of golf at this earliest known American muni is subject to a number of unique local rules that address special conditions affecting play, including Stolen Ball, Eaten Ball, Incinerated Ball, Ball Held for Ransom, Ball Embedded in Wet Concrete, Ball Soiled by Pigeons, Ball Struck in Flight by Stray Bullet, Ground Under Investigation, Flammable Obstruction, Suspicious Object, Casual Sewage, Gross Impediments, and Auto Parts Piled for Removal.

1897

Golf, the first magazine in America devoted entirely to the sport, begins publication. The monthly's premier issue features a short piece on the importance of the weight shift under the headline "A Revolutionary New Way to Swing the Club." A more or less verbatim version of the same article, under a variety of virtually identical titles, will appear in future issues of the popular periodical 109 times in the next 110 years.

1898

Coburn Haskell, an avid golfer from Cleveland, designs and patents the first golf ball with an inner rubber core surrounded by wound elastic threads and an outer layer of balata that provides a durable cover. Livelier and more forgiving than the solid "gutty," the new Haskell ball is quickly put into production by the Goodrich Rubber Company and is an immediate success, thanks to its superior playability out of bad lies and the greater length it travels regardless of whether it is hit well or poorly. Haskell is also the inventor of the rubber gas bags that make the modern blimp possible, and he implores Goodrich to construct one of the airships as a promotional tool "to hover in the skies above the venue of a golfing tournament, proudly displaying the name Goodrich in monumental lettering, thereby encouraging the purchase of the firm's excellent tires, and perhaps as well making a film of the proceedings with Mr. Edison's new Kinetoscope for later viewing by keen fans of the game." When Goodrich shows no enthusiasm for the project, Haskell demonstrates the singular lack of scruples that is

the most notable character trait of the true golfer by instantly peddling his idea to his erstwhile partner's archrival, Goodyear.

1899

First known use of the term "birdie" to refer to a score of 1 under par on a hole. The word appears to have been originated by a player named Ab Smith who hit what he described at the time as "a bird of a shot" that landed six inches from the hole and then went on to card what he and the other members of his threesome immediately took to calling a "birdie." Why this goofy usage caught on so fast is—like so much else in golf—a complete mystery, but there was a bright side to its nearly instant adoption. Any of the other contemporary slang alternatives would have saddled golfers forever after with even dopier descriptive words like "peachie," "dilly," "jim-dandy," "humdingie," "lollapaloosie," or "cat's pajamie."

II

DOWN THE FAIRWAY
1900–1957

1900

Harry Vardon wins the British and the U.S. Opens. The legendary English professional is best known today as the inventor of the classic overlapping "Vardon grip," but he was also the source of several other key golf innovations, among them the "Vardon tip" (a banknote delivered to the starter in a closed palm to get out ahead of a mixed foursome), the "Vardon nip" (a stealthy slug of whiskey imbibed from a hip flask before a key putt), and the "Vardon slip" (a well-timed visit to the bathroom to duck a clubhouse bar check). Sadly, he was also the unwilling originator of the tragic "Vardon yip," a nervous twitch that caused him to miss ridiculously short putts later in his career.

1901

Donald Ross constructs the first of three courses he will ultimately design at the famed Pinehurst Golf Resort, which now boasts five additional 18-hole layouts. Pinehurst No. 1 will be his inaugural effort in a long and celebrated career that will see the gifted architect create nearly five hundred courses. It's a truly impressive achievement, but this remarkable output constitutes only a small fraction of the more than seven thousand private clubs, public facilities, and resorts nationwide that currently claim to be the handiwork of the prolific Scot.

1902

Introduction of the first iron clubs with grooved faces. These linear scoring patterns incised into the metal striking surfaces make it possible for skilled golfers to impart the powerful backspin that causes their balls to "suck back" toward the hole when hit on the green, but offer little benefit for the average players who continue to hit shots that merely suck.

1903

Founding of the Oakmont Country Club, with a celebrated championship golf course laid out by Henry Fownes that is widely regarded as one of the finest examples of penal-style golf architecture. This concept of course design, which is one of the four basic schools of golf architecture, tests a golfer's ability to successfully execute a series of predetermined, stereotyped shots and punishes failure with the loss of at least one stroke for the experts and two or more for poor players. The other three schools are the strategic, epitomized early on in the work of "the four Willies" (Campbell, Davis, Dunn, and Park) and later by Donald Ross, Alister MacKenzie, and A. W. Tillinghast, which balances risks with rewards and puts a premium on thoughtful play by golfers of any skill level; the heroic, exemplified by the designs of Robert Trent Jones Sr. and Tom Fazio, which encourages bold play and favors the longer hitter but does not unduly penalize less accomplished golfers who elect to pursue a more cautious method of attack; and the idiotic, whose chief adherent is Pete Dye, which seeks to provide as miserable a golfing experience as possible to the largest number of players regardless of their degree of proficiency.

1904

Walter Travis becomes the first player from the United States to win the British Amateur Championship. English sports fans console themselves with the comforting thought that at least it wasn't a Frenchman.

1907

Arnaud Massy, a Frenchman, wins the British Open. English sports fans console themselves with the comforting thought that, after all, golf is still a man's game.

1908

Miss Charlotte Cecilia Pitcairn "Cecil" Leitch, an unknown seventeen-year-old girl with a strikingly modern, masculine-style golf swing who can regularly outdrive most men, reaches the semifinals of the Ladies Amateur Championship at St. Andrews, and Mrs. Gordon Robertson becomes the first female head pro at a golf club. English sports fans suddenly display a renewed interest in their island nation's other quirky, baffling, jargon-laden, homegrown, male-dominated ball game—cricket.

1909

Charles Blair MacDonald builds the National Golf Links in Southampton, many of whose eighteen holes are exact replicas of celebrated golf holes on famous links courses in England and Scotland. He thus singlehandedly invents a fifth distinct approach to course design that heavily influences the profession—the plagaristic or kleptomaniac school of golf architecture.

1910

The Royal and Ancient Golf Club of St. Andrews bans the center-shafted "Schenectady" mallet-headed putter used by Walter Travis in the 1904 British Amateur. The United States Golf Association refuses to endorse the ban, thereby creating a schism between the two self-appointed regulatory bodies that will last until 1952. The fact that there are effectively two separate sets of Rules of Golf proves awkward for professionals competing in events overseas, but the discord has very little impact on the vast majority of recreational golfers worldwide who are already playing according to a self-determined and self-regulating code of conduct that is noted for its inherent flexibility and leniency, and its generous spirit of uplift, recovery, and improvement.

1913

International play is inaugurated with a match between France and the United States at La Boulie, near Versailles, the first course with swans and ornamental fountains in its water hazards, topiary hedge sculptures along the fairways as yardage markers, and a halfway house with a Michelin star.

Twenty-year-old Francis Ouimet becomes the first amateur to win the U.S. Open, defeating the celebrated British professionals Harry Vardon and Ted Ray in a thrilling 18-hole play-off in Brookline, Massachusetts, the site some seven decades later of the notoriously partisan Ryder Cup of 1999. It certainly didn't hurt Ouimet's chances that as a hometown boy, he was an obvious crowd favorite, and it was probably no accident that Vardon and Ray routinely discovered that their wayward shots on the closing holes of the final round seemed to end up in uniformly and uniquely terrible lies. In fact, Vardon had to call for rulings when his ball was found stuck to the sole of a spectator's cleated shoe (he got a free drop), glued to the trunk of a tree with a wad of chewing gum (unplayable lie), and nestled in the core of a half-eaten candied apple (rub of the green), and Ray had to attempt more than once to hit his ball out from under an increasingly familiar-looking and strangely peripatetic rock.

1914

Formation of the Tokyo Golf Club at Komazawa, the first course with sword-wielding retired samurai warriors as course marshals, heated water hazards staffed with giggling geishas who serve as ball retrievers and golf-injury-relieving masseuses, and sand traps raked by Zen monks. The club is also credited with the first known golf haiku: "I tee up the ball. It just sits there. Why do I tremble?"

1916

The first miniature-golf course in the United States opens, in Pinehurst, North Carolina. The fabled Pinehurst No. ¼ still tops a list of all-time great "minis" that includes such minor masterpieces as Winged Toe, Spitballtusrol, Bantam Dunes, Smidgen Hills, Munchkin Ridge, Merionette, Hazelteeny, the Cuff Links at Spanish Bay, and the Doral Resort's legendary Blue Midget.

The Professional Golf Association of America is founded with eighty-two charter members, seventy-seven of whom call in sick or claim prior commitments to avoid having to play with the amateurs in the first pretournament Wednesday pro-am.

1918

Completion of the perennially top-rated Pine Valley Golf Club. Designer George Crump's spectacular layout in the sandy pine barrens of southern New Jersey is truly one of a kind, in that unlike most typical inland golf courses, which have bunkers, Pine Valley is a bunker that has a golf course.

1919

Pebble Beach Golf Links opens on the Monterey Peninsula. First four-dollar golf ball. First five-dollar beer. First six-hour round.

Publication of the first golf book to feature high-speed sequence photographs of the golf swing—*Picture Analysis of Golf Strokes* by Jim Barnes. Detailed records maintained by the USGA indicate that within six months of the instruction manual's appearance, the average handicap of American golfers increases by more than four full points, rising from its previous level of 17.4 to 21.8.

1920

The first practice range is opened, in Pinehurst. Introduction of the earliest-known mechanical ball-retrieving vehicle, a massive contraption based on World War I tank technology, with an armor-plated, shankproof, fully enclosed cab for the driver.

1922

The Walker Cup Match between British and American amateurs is instituted. The cup is named for George Herbert Walker, two of whose direct descendants would become the forty-first and forty-third presidents of the United States. In 2009, the Cup Committee will narrowly defeat a motion to rename the trophy awarded to the winning national team the Nitwit Cup.

Walter Hagen becomes the first native-born American to win the British Open. Unimpressed by the measly £75 prize money, Hagen, who made over $100,000 a year in product endorsements, private matches, and appearance fees, signed over the winner's check to his caddy on the spot. In another typically flamboyant gesture, Hagen, who as a mere golfing professional had been denied access to the facilities of the clubhouse at the Royal St. George's tournament site, parked a hired limousine in front of the club to use as a locker room and dining room during the tournament, and in a nose-thumbing parting shot, the Haig engaged a firm of master paper hangers in nearby Sandwich to TP the clubhouse from top to bottom the night he left with six hundred rolls of premium sanitary tissue.

Possibly inspired by the elegant root-and-crown structure of the teeth that are the focus of his profession, New Jersey dentist William Lowell patents the Reddy Tee, the classic wooden peg with a concave, funnel-shaped head that instantly becomes a standard and ubiquitous piece of golfing equipment. Its speedy adoption was due not just to its obvious utility, but also to an aggressive marketing campaign in which Walter Hagen was hired to promote the tees while touring. Hagen also deserves considerable credit for convincing the innovative orthodontist to replace his suggested names for the handy doohickey—"Easy-to-implant, Easy-to-extract Turf-perching Ball Molar" and "Graminaceous Bicuspid Dentoid Drive-Erecting Unit"—with the simpler and less alarming "golf tee."

Long treated as second-class golf citizens, public course players finally get their own tournament when the USGA launches the U.S. Amateur Public Links Championship. The annual competition is limited to golfers who are not currently members of any private club, and is conducted subject to several special rules tailor-made for the occasion: Entrants in the event who are not in their cars in the parking lot of the course where play is to take place at least six hours before their tee times are disqualified; a player may bribe the starter without endangering his own amateur status; there is no penalty for a lost ball if reasonable evidence exists that it is in fact a purloined ball; there is no penalty for hitting a wrong ball if the ball in question is being hit back at a group playing behind another group of players into which the trailing group hit a ball; and a club left lying on or near the green by a member of a previous playing group may be used by the player who finds it for the remainder of the round, or until the player who mislaid it returns to look for it, and if that player does not reclaim the club by the end of the round, it becomes the property of the player who found it.

1923

Opening of the Winged Foot Golf Club, whose renowned East and West Courses were designed by the famous—and famously hard-drinking—architect A. W. Tillinghast. The genius of "Terrible Tillie" is readily apparent in every hole of the twin 18s he laid out at Mamaroneck, but the thirsty genius's real passion was for the 19th, and the round-capping watering hole in Westchester is widely considered to be his masterpiece. Even the steadiest golfer is lucky to get away with nothing worse than a "double" as he navigates the long 4-or-more-shotter, with a massive bulkhead-style bar lining the left side of the narrow taproom, and then has to contend with a forced "carry" to a series of huge green-sized tabletops surrounded by overstuffed bucket-style chairs and deep settees covered with thick hassocks and defended by a low, curving wooden rail that leads to a tricky lower-level washroom treacherously positioned at the bottom of a sharply angled dogleg staircase.

1924

The first tubular steel club shafts are introduced and promptly legalized by the USGA, though the R&A will continue to ban them for several more years. The new metal sticks prove far superior in durability, consistency of feel, absence of torque, and reduction in wind resistance to the wooden shafts they quickly supplant. They also produce a somewhat more distracting sound when rattled during an opponent's backswing and, with practice, can be used to direct the sun into his eyes, but they do suffer from a few notable deficiencies. If tossed into a pond, they do not float, making their retrieval following a change of heart impractical; they cannot be burned in a fireplace in a heartwarming, score-settling blaze; they can be broken over the leg with a sharp downward motion or against a tree with a hammer blow, but they cannot be slowly bent to the breaking point with a steady and soul-soothing application of pressure, and at the moment of rupture, there is no satisfying *snap*, only a sort of weak *pop*; if left for a long period in the back of a garage, they will only rust, not rot, and no insect will eat them, making it harder to arrive at a final decision to take them to the dump; and no matter how long they are kept, they never attain the status of valuable antiques likely to be coveted by deep-pocketed collectors—they always remain just a bunch of crummy old clubs.

1925

The Brook Hollow Golf Club in Dallas installs the first complete fairway irrigation system. First complaints about brown spots and burned-out areas. First out-of-the blue sunny-day soakings of surprised foursomes. First tournament-day sprinkler-head blowouts. First summer fungus in Texas.

1926

Texan Kenneth Smith devises a pair of handy equipment-testing tools, the Lorhythmic Swingweight Scale, which supplies a standard measure of the distribution of weight among the components of the new metal-shafted clubs to permit the manufacture of custom-made matched sets by assigning them a range of values from A-0 (the lightest) to E-9 (the heaviest), and the Loballistic Flingweight Gauge, which provides a comparative assessment of the maximum distance any given club can be thrown, with ratings running from Bronze (less than 50 feet), to Silver (upward of 75 feet), and Gold (over 100 feet).

Walter Hagen plays Bobby Jones in a privately sponsored 72-hole challenge match in Florida billed as the "World Championship." After losing to Hagen by a decisive margin of 12 and 11 despite the Haig's notorious wildness off the tee, an exasperated Jones complains that "when a man misses his drive, and then misses with his second shot, and then wins the hole with a birdie, it gets my goat." Never at a loss for words, the dapper Sir Walter allows a small smile to play across his face, gives a courtly bow, and with a twinkle in his eye slyly retorts, "Kiss my ass, Bo-Jo."

1927

The first official Ryder Cup Match between the American and British and Irish teams takes place at Worcester Country Club and is won convincingly by the U.S. side with a score of 9½ to 2½. In contrast to some of the more recent stagings of the biennial event, an atmosphere of sportsmanship prevailed throughout the contest, as competitors on both sides generously pointed out flaws and idiosyncrasies in each other's swings, went out of their way to call their opponents' attention to a few things that could go wrong that they might not have thought of as they prepared to hit critical shots, and routinely conceded putts when the ball in question could not be marked without the coin falling into the cup.

Introduction of creeping bent grass for putting surfaces, thereby fulfilling one of the enduring goals of the recently established turf research section of the USGA—unputtable greens. Its two other major objectives—unplayable rough and tight-as-a-drum closely mown fairways that are impossible to hit a wood or long iron off of—will have to wait for the development of specially bred mutant grass strains in the 1970s and 1980s.

1928

Cypress Point Golf Club opens on the Monterey Peninsula. No one plays the spectacular oceanside Alister MacKenzie course for almost three years, when all of the prospective members of the superprivate, ultraexclusive club blackball each other in a bitter and unseemly standoff that comes to an end only in 1931 when the financial pressures of the Great Depression finally break the ugly deadlock.

1929

Bobby Jones holes what is still considered the greatest putt ever made under tournament pressure—a 12-foot, downhill, double-breaking snake on the 18th green at Winged Foot in the final hole of the U.S. Open to force a playoff with Al Espinosa, whom he easily beat the following day. Jones always attributed his miraculous save to his famous putter, Calamity Jane, which he had wisely substituted just a few weeks earlier for its unproductive predecessors, Little Miss Muffet, No, No, Nanette, Runaround Sue, and the Unsinkable Molly Brown.

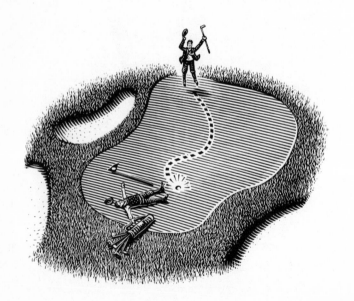

The two leading women players of the time—six-time U.S. Amateur winner Glenna Collett and four-time British Ladies champion Joyce Wethered—compete one last time for the British Ladies Championship. The epic 36-hole match at St. Andrews between the two great transatlantic rivals seesawed back and forth several times before Joyce Wethered finally prevailed on the 35th hole, winning the storied 17th "Road Hole" to seal the victory 3-and-1. Both players married shortly after the historic encounter, and both went on to establish annual awards for lady golfers in the new husbands' names. Glenna Collett (Mrs. Edwin Vare) inaugurated the Vare Trophy for lowest stroke average per round, and Joyce Wethered (Lady Heathcoat-Amory) instituted the Heathcoat-Amory Medallion for nicest shoes.

After the Prince of Wales is observed playing golf with steel-shafted clubs at St. Andrews, the R&A quickly rescinds its ban on the new equipment, rightly fearing that any attempt to enforce it on the golf-crazed future king will inevitably result in the issuance of a decree on his coronation day revoking the organization's enviable

designation as the Royal and Ancient Golf Club of St. Andrews and replacing it with some less laudatory title, like the Disloyal and Senile Golf Club of St. Andrews, the Vile and Asinine Golf Club of St. Andrews, or the Dumb and Dumber Golf Club of St. Andrews.

1930

Bobby Jones registers the game's greatest achievement by completing the Grand Slam of golf—victories in both the U.S. and British Amateurs and the U.S. and British Opens in a single calendar year. Incredibly, the widely reported feat does not represent the totality of his golfing accomplishments in this annus mirabilis. He later confided to his biographer, O. B. Keeler, that to relieve the tension of competing in the last two legs of the "Impregnable Quadrilateral"—the U.S. Open at Interlachen in Minneapolis and the U.S. Amateur at Merion in Pennsylvania—he had donned dark glasses and a fake mustache and entered, and won, the U.S. Miniature-Golf Tournament then under way at nearby Mini-Ap'o'Links and, a few weeks later, the U.S. Long-Drive Contest held at a practice range close to Merion in Conshohocken. He also admitted to Keeler, somewhat sheepishly, that the slight bulge on the right side of his jacket in the famous photograph that shows him posing with the trophies of the four majors was caused by the two additional minor awards he'd slipped into his pocket—a small, hood-ornament-sized silver statuette of the Winged Victory of Samothrace for the U.S. Miniature and a six-inch-long gold-plated tee for the 259-yard wallop with a hickory-shafted driver that secured him the title America's Biggest Hitter.

1931

Convinced that he has accomplished everything he set out to do in competitive golf, and exhausted by the ferocious pressure of tournament play, Bobby Jones retires, but not before making his greatest and most lasting contribution to the game—the "Thousand-Grand Slam"—by accepting $1 million to endorse a matched set of Robert T. Jones Jr. golf clubs to be manufactured by Spalding. He also makes eighteen instructional films, begins writing the first of four bestselling books, and helps design and oversees construction of the Augusta National golf course, the future home of the Masters. Thus, in a single year, he has created from scratch the entire quartet of tour-winnings-supplementing income sources that will turn even journeyman pros of the future into millionaires: apparel and equipment promotion, golf instruction, course design, and tournament hosting—golf's immortal and astonishingly profitable "Incomparable Quadruple."

1932

Repeating half of Jones's phenomenal sweep, Gene Sarazen wins both the U.S. and British Opens, but that sterling performance pales in comparison with his other great contribution to the game in the same year—the invention of the sand wedge. The club's heavy flange exploits the principle of the wing to permit skilled players to execute magical shots, exploding a ball out of a bunker on a thin layer of sand and deftly lofting even a fried egg to a soft landing within inches of the cup. Alas, in the hands of a hacker, the thick-edged, bottom-weighted club has a tendency to demonstrate a pair of other less useful physical laws—the principle of the hockey stick, producing stinging slap shots that rocket off into space, or the principle of the backhoe, digging a series of gouges and furrows or excavating a more or less continuous trench, in either case without significantly altering the position of the ball. Recognizing this unfortunate state of affairs, the ingenious—and generous—Sarazen devises a pair of additional playing aids specifically designed for the long-suffering duffer: a lightweight, portable, extendable sixteen-foot telescoping ball retriever and a score-keeping pencil with an eraser on the end.

In a potentially huge contribution to the enjoyment of the game by the average golfer, the English surgeon and gifted amateur golfer Dr. Frank Stableford devises an elegant and easy-to-use scoring system that awards 4 points for an eagle, 3 for a birdie, 2 for a par, 1 for a bogey, and zero for anything worse than a bogey, thus making the player with the highest score—the one with the most points—the winner. This simple, fair, and eminently sensible method of tabulating strokes speeds play and encourages wider participation in the sport by providing the maximum opportunity for thrilling, risk-taking shots while eliminating the frustration of a catastrophic "blow-up" hole or a depressing string of double bogeys. Golf being golf, the Stableford System is almost never used.

1933

The Hershey Chocolate Company hosts the Hershey Open, becoming golf's first corporate sponsor and inaugurating the seemingly endless parade of two-bit, second-tier, nonblimpworthy tournaments that will provide bread-and-butter playing opportunities to no-name touring pros in the years to come, as well as a crucial source of much-needed, if vapid, diversion for generations of bored and desperate rained-out golfers.

1934

The great American amateur Lawson Little duplicates the other half of Jones's slam, winning both the U.S. and British Amateurs, a bravura performance he will repeat the following year. Little often had as many as twenty-five clubs in his bag, supplementing the traditional mashie, niblick, mashie-niblick, sammy, blaster, and jigger irons and the brassie, baffie, cleek, and spoon woods with a dazzling array of weaponry, including a bashie, a lashie, a smashie, a slashie, a buster, a wedgie, a whammy, a hickey, a noogie, a hickey-noogie, a noodnick, a moishe-schmendrick, a snigger, a flogger, and a fiddlestick, and a daffie, a half-assie, a demi-tassie, a buffoon, a spontoon, a Brigadoon, and a geek. His long-suffering caddie, Eddie "Swayback" Pinella was one of the founders of the International Union of Bag Carriers and Club Luggers, whose lobbying efforts helped persuade the USGA to pass a rule establishing a fourteen-club maximum four years later.

1935

Gene Sarazen puts the new Masters' Tournament on the golfing map and gives the whole game a huge boost when he scores an amazing double eagle on the par-5 15th hole at Augusta, holing a 4-wood for a deuce with "the shot heard round the world." His historic albatross is unequaled until the 1960s when Liam Higgins takes advantage of a gale force tailwind to make a hole in one on the dogleg par-4 16th at Waterville in Ireland, and Kim Il Sung, the multitalented Great Leader of North Korea, adds to his lifetime list of heroic triumphs by reportedly carding an impressive, if inexplicable, "goose egg" hole in none for a score of zero on the par-3 fifth at Workers Paradise Valley in Pyongyang.

Golf-crazy tinkerer Eddie Stimpson invents a simple device for calculating green speeds. His basic design—a three-foot-long grooved inclined plane that releases a golf ball at a twenty-degree angle and a tape measure to record the number of feet it rolls—is perfected some forty years later by USGA tech wizard Frank Thomas, and the Stimpmeter is now a standard piece of greenkeeping equipment. Stimpson dreamed up two other nifty gizmos, which, sad to say, have long since been forgotten: the Stimputer, an easy-to-use apparatus similar to a slide rule for calculating the markup on items in the pro shop, and the Stimpograph, a crude but surprisingly effective lie detector with a galvanic hygrometer that measured the amount of moisture on a golfer's palms to determine the veracity of the handicap he claimed to be playing off.

1936

John Fischer wins the U.S. Amateur, becoming the last golfer to achieve victory in a major championship while playing with hickory-shafted clubs. A die-hard golfing purist, Fischer also used golf tees he whittled from twigs; wore hobnail boots, a pith helmet, a muslin golf glove, and tweed underwear; had a burlap and tarpaulin golf bag with a horsehair bag towel; kept track of the time with a small sundial mounted on a wristband; marked his ball with a thumb tack; and entered his score on a clay tablet with a bronze stylus.

1937

The team of American professionals scores the first U.S. victory in a Ryder Cup Match played in Britain, commencing a period of almost total dominance of the event by the Yankee upstarts that will last until the British and Irish side is expanded some four decades later to include players from the entire European Union. Discouraged by the endless string of defeats, Samuel Ryder, the wealthy seed magnate who originally donated the cup that bears his name, proposes that three additional sports—darts, skittles, and snooker—be included in the competition to provide a fairer test of national skills. The Americans

counter with a recommendation to widen the scope of the tournament with contests in bass fishing, tag-team wrestling, and hot dog eating. It is mutually decided to stick to golf.

1938

Ralph Guldahl, the unsung contemporary of fellow Texans Ben Hogan and Byron Nelson, takes the second of two consecutive U.S. Open titles, becoming the last golfer to win the tournament while wearing a necktie. In his brief career, the old-school Dallas professional also recorded several other "lasts," including being the last player to ensure that his nails were cleaned and trimmed before he gave a heckler the finger, the last player to fill out and present to his caddie official, profanity-laced complaint forms whenever he wanted to blame him for some mishap, and the last player to call opponents he disliked formal names like Mister Buttwipe, Mister Dickhead, and Mister Slimeball.

1939

Still smarting from their defeat at the hands of the American golfers, the English declare war on Germany, using the excuse of the onset of hostilities to cancel the next four Ryder Cups.

1940

Texas club pro Jimmy Demaret, a notoriously colorful dresser with a fondness for golfing outfits in iridescent shades of red and green, wins at Augusta, becoming the first—and last—Masters champion who does not visibly flinch when he dons the coveted but revolting ceremonial green jacket.

1942

In order to conserve vital resources for the campaign to defeat Germany and Japan, the U.S. government orders a halt to the manufacture of golf equipment for the duration of the war, and major club makers waste no time retooling for the war effort. Spalding produces the Shure-Shot K.O. Kraut Krusher 3" mortar, and Wilson turns out an 81-mm version of the same weapon, the Zippy Zapper Jap Blaster. Interestingly, both of the lightweight artillery pieces display the same wayward shot pattern, firing shells that tend to land short and to the right.

1943

Baffled and irritated by their inability to convince the warring powers to get their priorities straight and cease all hostilities forthwith, the members of Augusta National reluctantly cancel the Masters.

1945

Byron Nelson wins eleven consecutive PGA tournaments, establishing a streak of victories that is one of the very few professional golf records Tiger Woods is unlikely to equal or surpass. The others are: losing in a string of playoffs in all four major championships (Craig Wood and Greg Norman); blowing a major tournament with the worst score on the finishing hole (Sam Snead, an 8, in the 1939 U.S. Open); and carding the highest recorded score on any one hole of a PGA-sanctioned tournament (Ed "Porky" Oliver, a double-snowman 16, on the 16th hole at Cypress Point in the 1954 Crosby).

1946

Pressed by his longtime friend and fellow competitor, John Bulla, Sam Snead reluctantly enters, and then proceeds to win, the British Open at St. Andrews. Though ultimately victorious in the prestigious championship, Snead gets off on the wrong foot right from the start when he spots the legendary links from his train window and wonders aloud if it is "an old abandoned golf course." He subsequently makes no effort to disguise his dislike of the course, his hotel, the food, his caddie, the town, and its people, and he also makes it clear that he has no intention of returning to Britain the following year to defend his title, which he thinks little of and whose Royal and Ancient sponsors he obviously loathes. The feeling is apparently mutual. When he gets back home to West Virginia and unpacks the special carrying case in which the tournament trophy was shipped, he discovers that it does not contain the heavy silver replica of the famous Claret Jug traditionally awarded to Open champions, but rather a galvanized steel canister filled with two quarts of sheep dip. The Royal and Ancient later apologizes for the regrettable mix-up and by way of atonement sends Snead a beer mug, a hat, and a bag towel with the town seal of St. Andrews; a place mat, a tray, and a platter with scenes of the Old Course; and a voucher good for one free night at any local bed-and-breakfast.

1947

After several years as a top U.S. woman professional golfer, the great female athlete and former Olympic track and field star Mildred "Babe" Didrikson Zaharias successfully petitions the USGA to restore her amateur status. She takes two U.S. Amateur titles in quick succession, followed by a series of fifteen straight tournament victories, culminating in her singular triumph in the British Ladies Championship at Gullane in Scotland, when she became the first American ever to win the event. Having clearly established herself as the finest woman golfer in the world, Zaharias accepts $300,000 to make some short movies and once again turns professional. She goes on to win three U.S. Women's Opens as an LPGA star, thereby gaining not only a well-deserved payday and further recognition but also a unique standing as the only player who, in a pinch, can, all by herself, fill in for an entire missing foursome in a charity pro-am golf tournament.

The first of the great South African golfers, Arthur D'Arcy "Bobby" Locke, begins playing on the U.S. PGA tour and proceeds to win eleven tournaments in a two-and-a-half year period, including the Chicago Victory

National by 16 strokes, which tied the all-time PGA tour record for a tournament victory margin. Barred from the U.S. tour on specious grounds (simply put, he was a foreigner and he was winning too often), Locke went on to play in Great Britain, where he won the British Open four times. A natural right-to-left player whose basic shot bordered on a hook, he is widely considered one of the greatest putters of all time, even though he also hooked his putts. He is the author of golf's most famous phrase—"Drive for show, putt for dough"—as well as a number of less well-known but equally shrewd pieces of golfing wisdom, including: "After the first putt sinks, the hole shrinks," "Every putt is a straight putt if you hit the damn thing hard enough," "Spike marks never turn a putt toward the cup," "No putt ever got longer as a result of being marked," "A golf match is a test of your skill against your opponent's dumb luck," "You can draw the ball, you can fade the ball, but no one can straight the ball," and "Follow your dreams, except for that one where you show up for a golf tournament naked."

1948

At the age of forty-one, one of the greatest English players of the prewar period, Henry Cotton, wins his third British Open, setting a new course record of 66 in his second round at Muirfield. In an effort to attract sponsorship money during the lean postwar years, the wellborn but spendthrift "Maestro" of the links seeks to translate his triumph into an apparel endorsement contract by offering to change his name to Henry Nylon, Henry Banlon, Henry Orlon, Henry Rayon, Henry Dacron, Henri Piquet, Harry Polyester, Hari Madras, Enrico Viyella, Enrique Vicuña, or Hank Doubleknit. There are no takers.

1949

After barely surviving a terrible automobile accident that left him so badly injured that it was feared he might never walk again, let alone play golf, Ben Hogan is sidelined for the entire season. In his longtime rival's absence, Sam Snead has his best year ever, winning the Masters, the PGA, and the Western Open, and coming in second in the U.S. Open at Medinah, one stroke behind Cary Middlecoff. After several rounds of celebratory cocktails, Middlecoff's caddie tells a group of golf journalists that he saw an amazingly lifelike, two-foot-tall voodoo doll of Ben Hogan with several dozen needles stuck in its legs in Snead's locker, but later retracts his story under pressure from the PGA and retires from the tour a month later to run the prosperous chicken farm he just inherited upon the untimely death of a long-lost relative.

The Ladies Professional Golf Association, led by its energetic and enterprising tournament manager, Fred Corcoran, replaces a number of floundering competing organizations, including the Women's Professional Golf Association, the Gals' Professional Golf Association, the Dames' Professional Golf Association, the Dolls' Professional Golf Association, the Broads' Professional Golf Association, the Chicks' Professional Golf Association, and the Tomatoes' Professional Golf Association.

1950

In one of the greatest comebacks in golf history, Ben Hogan returns to the tour a year after his nearly fatal car accident. He loses to Snead in a play-off in the Los Angeles Open, but even in defeat, he unknowingly obtains a critical advantage when a rules-obsessed gypsy in the gallery surrounding the 18th green at Riviera spots Snead employing an amulet concealed in his palm to put a jinx on Hogan and decides that any such talisman, fetish, or charm is an Artificial Device or Unusual Equipment whose use should have led to Snead's immediate disqualification. Employing his sorcerer's skills to rectify the situation as best as he can, the passionate Romany golfing fan quietly casts a counterspell that unwinds the curse, and for good measure gives Snead the evil eye. Hogan goes on to win the U.S. Open at Merion, and the Open remains the one major tournament Snead will never capture in his long career.

1951

Continuing his courageous recovery, Ben Hogan wins the U.S. Open at Oakland Hills, remarking with obvious satisfaction at the posttournament award ceremonies, "I vowed I would bring this monster to its knees."

The "monster" in question is the dull but demanding Donald Ross layout that the USGA hired noted architect Robert Trent Jones to lengthen and toughen to whatever degree was necessary to ensure that the winning score was no better than par. It is the first of what will be many such overhauls undertaken over the course of the next half century by Jones and his gifted son Rees at the behest of the USGA in their roles as "U.S. Open course doctors" charged with the task of turning classic old venues into nightmarish Frankenlinks. Still, there is a limit to what even the most inspired designer can accomplish in an age when foot-tall rough, ten-yard-wide fairways, two-acre bunkers, and supersonic burned-out greens are not enough to deter the likes of Tiger Woods, and it is widely understood that given the USGA's maniacal obsession with defending par, it is only a matter of time before the 600-yard par-5s, the 500-yard-plus par-4s, and the 295-yard par-3s will be joined by formidable 200-yard par-2s and punishing 160 yard par-1s.

The USGA and the R&A convene a conference that ultimately issues a revised and almost totally standardized version of the Rules of Golf. The stymie is abolished, the center-shafted putter is legalized, and the penalty of stroke and distance for balls hit out of bounds is agreed upon. The only remaining areas of disagreement are the dimensions of the ball (the American ball is a minimum of 1.68" in diameter, the British ball is 1.62"); the temperature of the draft beer in club taprooms (in the United States, a maximum of 48°, in the United Kingdom, 74°); the minimum thickness of towels in the locker room (U.S., 1/8", U.K., 1/64"); the size of tips for caddies and clubhouse personnel (U.S., 10–15%, U.K., 1–1 ½ %); the length of the standard gimme (U.S., 38", U.K., 11"); and the number of mulligans allowed per round (U.S., 4, U.K., 0).

1952

Ignoring numerous death threats, groundbreaking African-American professional Charlie Sifford enters the Phoenix Open. When he and the other black members of his playing group reach the first green, they find that the cup has been filled with excrement. It is only the first of the many hundreds of shitty golf holes that will one day blanket the state of Arizona.

1953

In a fitting start to the next half century of network broadcast coverage of golf, the World Golf Championship becomes the first nationally televised golf tournament, and in a suitably thrilling finish, Lew Worsham hits one of the game's most unforgettable shots, holing out from 135 yards to eagle the final hole and win the event by one stroke during a commercial for Ovaltine.

Eisenhower is elected president. A passionate golfer who regularly scored in the mid-80s, Ike does much to popularize a sport formerly considered elitist. He is seen on the golf course so often while in office that his cottage at Augusta National is popularly known as "the little White House" and the White House, where he has hired Robert Trent Jones to install a practice putting green, is generally referred to as "the big Halfway House." Although he successfully launched the interstate highway system, a deeply frustrated Eisenhower fails to convince the penny-pinching Congress to cough up the $1 billion price tag for a companion nationwide interstate fairway system of more than a thousand municipal golf courses located near major interchanges of the new expressways. Interestingly, some three decades later, Alabama resurrects the idea on a somewhat smaller scale, hiring Robert Trent Jones to design a series of eleven courses (468 holes) across the state that became known as the Robert Trent Jones Golf Trail.

Ben Hogan captures three of the four titles that comprise the modern Grand Slam: the Masters, the U.S. Open at Oakmont, and the British Open at Carnoustie. Hogan's historic sweep is made all the sweeter when he contemplates the somewhat less impressive Sammy Slam achieved by his rival, Sam Snead, in the same season: the Baton Rouge Open, the Greenbrier Pro-Am, and the Orlando Two-Ball.

Peter Alliss, who in later years would gain fame as a long-winded BBC British Open golf commentator with a penchant for tut-tutting players' missed putts, takes 4 strokes to get down from the edge of the green on the 36th hole of the Ryder Cup at Wentworth, losing to Jim Turnesa. The limey gasbag's titanic four-jack costs Great Britain the cup, an epic meltdown that the plummy-tonsiled motormouth never seems to recollect during decades of history-dredging bloviation as anchor of the Beeb's TV coverage of the biennial event.

1955

In one of the biggest upsets in golf history, Jack Fleck, a total unknown, edges out Ben Hogan in a play-off to win the U.S. Open at San Francisco's Olympic Golf Club. Fleck joins the previous year's no-name champion, Ed Furgol, and such other past and future flash-in-the-pan low-wattage luminaries as Olin Dutra, Sam Parks, Tony Manero, Lloyd Mangrum, Dick Mayer, Orville Moody, Lou Graham, Hubert Green, Andy North, Steve Jones, and Lucas Glover on the USGA's honor roll of unlikely winners, a list that calls into question the organization's oft-stated claim that the severe course setups it favors are meant "not to embarrass the best players, but to identify them."

Life magazine pays Ben Hogan $20,000 for revealing the "secret" of how he got rid of his hook. Sadly for duffers everywhere, Henry Luce balks at Hogan's demand for a further $20 million to reveal the secret of how to get rid of a slice.

1956

Cary Middlecoff, a dentist who abandoned his profession to pursue a hugely successful career as a professional golfer, follows up his pervious year's victory at the Masters with his second U.S. Open title. An excruciatingly slow player, Middlecoff is nevertheless an exceptionally thoughtful and considerate competitor, and drawing on a time-honored tradition from his former dental practice, he always has several well-thumbed, two-year-old copies of golf magazines in his bag for his opponents to peruse during the seemingly interminable waits between his shots.

1957

Even though yip-prone blathermeister Peter Alliss is a member of the squad, the Great Britain and Ireland team captained by Welshman Dai Rees manages to eke out its first Ryder Cup victory over the American players since 1933. It will also be their last until the English-speaking countries seek admission to the European Union in a shameless but ultimately successful ploy to add Seve Ballesteros to the team.

III

ONTO THE GREEN

1958–1992

1958

Arnold Palmer wins the first of his four Masters titles. With his charisma, engaging personality, common-man background, bold play, and made-for-TV good looks, the hugely popular Palmer will almost single-handedly transform the game of golf from a sport enjoyed by a few thousand inept upper-crust country club hackers who can't break 100 to a sport enjoyed by millions of inept middle-class public course hackers who can't break 100.

At the age of twenty-three, Mickey Wright, one of the greatest women golfers of all time, wins the U.S. Women's Open and the LPGA Championship. In a career lasting only slightly more than fifteen years, Wright scores victories in eighty-two tournaments, thirteen of them majors, yet her name and that of her equally gifted contemporary, Kathy Whitworth, and their distinguished LPGA predecessors, Patty Berg, Louise Suggs, and the Bauer sisters, are virtually unknown today. The relative obscurity of these remarkable champions is directly attributable to a pair of nearly insurmountable obstacles that stand in the way of a wider appreciation of their chosen sport: It does not take place on a beach, and the players do not wear bikinis.

1959

In spite of a double bogey that reduces the intense perfectionist to tears, Gary Player wins the British Open at Muirfield. The supremely self-confident South African will go on to win the Masters, the PGA, and the U.S. Open, becoming one of only five golfers ever to achieve the career Grand Slam. A tireless worker, and a dedicated and outspoken diet, health, and fitness fanatic, Player is known as "the Black Knight" because of his custom of dressing entirely in black, a fashion choice he bases on his firm conviction that the dark fabric will permit him to directly assimilate the sun's energy. (He is also rumored to have his golf spikes regularly demagnetized to avoid a buildup of negative polarity that might inhibit his leg movement and to use lead-lined clubhead covers to protect his driver and fairway woods from distance-robbing impacts from high-energy subatomic particles—a pair of quirky habits that earn him the additional sobriquet "the Black Nut.") His appearance on the golf scene marks the midpoint of a gradual but inexorable transition from the previous era of self-taught, salt-of-the-earth, chain-smoking, hard-drinking, poorly paid club pros who happen to be able to putt to the current generation of clean-living, Bible-thumping, tax-dodging, nose-to-the-grindstone, by-the-book, millionaire gym rats who happen to be able to putt.

Jack Nicklaus, the player who will soon become Arnold Palmer's historic rival and who will ultimately be recognized as the greatest golfer of all time, wins the first of two consecutive U.S. Amateur titles. Incredibly, the immensely talented son of a successful Ohio pharmacist initially gives serious consideration to remaining an amateur in an attempt to emulate Bobby Jones's career as a sportsman, but he quickly concludes that there are several million compelling reasons why this is not a sensible plan.

1960

Arnold Palmer has his finest year, winning the Masters and the U.S. Open in thrilling finishes, coming in second in the British Open, and scoring victories in six other PGA events. He also makes one of the greatest plays of his lifetime by signing up as the first client of sports superagent Mark McCormack, thereby obtaining virtually all of the considerable benefits he would have received had he sold his soul to the devil without having to suffer the considerable downside of spending all eternity in hell.

1961

Arnold Palmer wins the first of a pair of back-to-back British Open titles. His decision to invest the time and effort necessary to compete in the overseas championship in spite of its meager purse and often trying playing conditions convinces other American players to include the event in their schedules, thus probably rescuing the venerable tournament from oblivion. The grateful Brits offer him a knighthood, but he politely declines the honor, explaining that it would represent a considerable comedown from his current status as "the King."

A mere century after the Emancipation Proclamation, the PGA of America finally gets around to eliminating the shameful Caucasians-only clause from its bylaws, permitting African-American professionals to become members of the association for the first time. In a move the organization will later come to regret, the PGA fails, however, to replace the offensive language with a different, and far more defensible, "earthlings only" clause, resulting in the inevitable takeover of the game of golf just a few decades later by long-driving, low-scoring, steely nerved space aliens who begin arriving on our planet in the early 1990s from a little-known golfing mecca in a star system on the edge of the Crab Nebula.

1962

The rookie professional Jack Nicklaus defeats local favorite Arnold Palmer in a memorable play-off in the U.S. Open at Oakmont. Palmer rebounds with victories at the Masters and the British Open, but Nicklaus will dominate American golf over the next two decades. Still, when all is said and done, Palmer will leave the more lasting legacy as the first player to have his own quasi-military force (Arnie's Army), the only player to be mentioned in a James Bond film (*Goldfinger*) and an episode of a TV series (*MacGyver*), the only celebrity other than Shirley Temple to have a nonalcoholic beverage named after him (the Arnold Palmer—half lemonade and half iced tea), the only player to own a piece of Pebble Beach, and the only player to be featured as the punch line in a classic golf joke involving God.

1963

Club manufacturers perfect the casting method for fabricating irons, making possible larger clubs with a wider sweet spot, thicker soles, and better weight distribution than traditional forged blades. These more forgiving sets feature a deeply inset cavity-back clubhead rather than the typical flat muscle-back design of hammered-steel clubs; they generally produce better results even when the ball is mishit; and when they fail to live up to their billing as "game improvement clubs," they can be thrown an average of ten yards farther than the old-fashioned implements.

1964

Somehow managing to stay upright during the 36-hole final round on the last day of play at the blisteringly hot Congressional Country Club near Washington, an obviously dazed and debilitated Ken Venturi overcomes a severe case of heat prostration to win the U.S. Open by 4 strokes. Clearly impressed by the doughty pro's ability to function under pressure while in a semiconscious state, CBS soon afterward taps Venturi to be a color commentator for their live TV golf coverage, and over the next thirty-five years the often befuddling game analyst validates the network's confidence by maintaining impressive Nielsen rating numbers even during the most marginal tournaments, filling endless hours of on-air downtime with puzzling anecdotes, dizzy observations, and noggin-numbing pronouncements that immobilize the millions of viewers who slump stunned and stupefied on their sofas, the suddenly leaden remote slipping from their limp and lifeless hands.

1965

The brash young ball-crushing phenom, Jack Nicklaus, wins the tradition-laden Masters by a whopping 9 strokes, blowing away the opposition and demolishing the storied Augusta National golf course with a record-setting 72-hole score of 271. His unprecedented performance prompts a flabbergasted Bobby Jones to remark that Nicklaus "plays a game with which I am not familiar." The nonplussed but always erudite golfing legend went on to observe, somewhat acidly, that the casually dressed and obsessively deliberate twenty-five-year-old also "plays that particular game of his attired in clothes dead in which I would not be caught, and at a snaillike pace up with which I would not put."

The PGA establishes the first Qualifying School, the brutal annual multiround tournament known familiarly as Q-School attended by professionals seeking to earn or retain the all-important card that confers playing privileges on the Tour. At the same time, the organization inaugurates a less well-known but equally demanding P's and Q's etiquette school where prospective Tour players are tested on their mastery of basic top-pro deportment, including the ability to remain in some form of continuous, methodical, and marginally purposeful motion on a green for a minimum of three minutes while studying a putt from at least four separate heights and angles; the concentration it takes to remember to perform a right-shoulder sleeve tug before every key shot; the lip control necessary to clearly and unmistakably mouth the "f---" and "s---" words without making any detectable sound; the dexterity required to scrawl a semilegible autograph on twenty cap bills with a Sharpie in under thirty sec-

onds; the speaking skills called for in the inevitable midround interview that includes the phrases "play my own game," "stay focused," "stay positive," "stay patient and give myself chances," "make the most of the scoring opportunities," "go low," "play within myself," and "go out there and have fun"; and the exquisite timing needed to execute a major-league crotch scratch and hack up a colossal gob of spit the exact instant a TV camera moves in for a close-up.

1966

Billy Casper, an underrated player overshadowed by his superstar contemporaries Arnold Palmer, Gary Player, and Jack Nicklaus, demonstrates an unmatched wizardry with the flat stick as he takes only 117 putts over 90 holes to defeat Palmer in a play-off and win his second U.S. Open. Casper won the Masters four years later, and went on to become personal golf instructor to King Hassan II of Morocco. It was in that capacity that he witnessed one of the game's most unique and least repeatable record-setting performances when, following a failed coup attempt by military officers who planned to attack the sovereign as he played on the links, the irked monarch had 59 shot at the Royal Dar es Salaam golf course.

1967

Going into the final round of the U.S. Open tied with Arnold Palmer and Billy Casper, Jack Nicklaus shoots a 65 to win the event by 4 strokes, beating the previous record for a low tournament scoring total set by Ben Hogan at Riviera two decades earlier. His victorious performance at Baltusrol also marked Nicklaus's emergence from Arnold Palmer's shadow as a popular and respected golfing figure in his own right and showcased his new and more presentable personal appearance after a single-minded makeover. Determined to shed the prevailing prior perception of the hugely talented player as a burly, callow slob with a crew cut that earned him the hostility of Arnie's adoring fans and the toxic moniker "Fat Jack," Nicklaus has slimmed down, opted for a snazzier wardrobe, and let his hair grow into the telltale blond mane that will become his trademark. He also spent hours huddled with his handlers in an effort to devise a new persona with a crowd-friendly nickname, and after wisely rejecting a number of ill-advised descriptive concepts, including "the Yellow Subparmachine," "Big Birdier," "the Sunflower Powerhouse," "the Dandy Lion," "The Focused Crocus," "the Saffron Basher," and "the 18-Karat Kid," they finally settle on the winning image that will become both an increasingly fond nickname and a highly successful corporate logo—"the Golden Bear."

Catherine Lacoste, daughter of the French tennis champion René Lacoste, who founded the noted Lacoste sportswear company, becomes the first and thus far the only amateur player ever to win the U.S. Women's Open. At the awards ceremony, she explains for the umpteenth time, to no avail, that the little lizard logo on her polo shirt is a crocodile, not an alligator.

1968

In one of the sorriest episodes in the annals of the game, Roberto De Vicenzo signs an incorrect scorecard at the end of the final round of the Masters, and even though the scorekeeping error was made by his playing partner, Tommy Aaron, and increased, rather than lowered his shot total, the one-stroke penalty for the infraction costs him the chance for an 18-hole play-off with Bob Goalby, who wins the green jacket by default. The gentlemanly Argentine player accepts the decision stoically with the unforgettable lament, "What a stupid I am," adding under his breath, "What a bag for the douching he is," when Goalby resists any suggestion of a sporting resolution to the sad state of affairs. By way of consolation, chagrined tournament chairman Cliff Roberts later sends De Vicenzo one of the club's deluxe, ultraplush padded-velvet green coat hangers, a packet of little green mothballs, and an official, members-only Augusta National pink-petal-azalea squirting-flower gag boutonniere with a side pocket, half-pint squeeze-bulb water reservoir connected to the novelty rubber buttonhole blossom by a three-foot length of flexible, color-coordinated, forest-green plastic tubing.

Plagued by a classic case of late-career yips, Sam Snead hits upon the idea of putting croquet-style, swinging the putter between his legs like a mallet as he stands with his feet on either side of the line of the putt. The USGA promptly bans the method as contrary to golf tradition, and probably would have put the kibosh on the tactic no matter what, but Slammin' Sammy does not help make the case for his novel technique when, obviously bored and distracted in a forgettable exhibition match, his ball hits another player's ball on a green. He then absent-mindedly walks over, places his ball directly behind and touching the ball he hit, puts his foot on it, and whacks the back of it with a one-handed hammer blow, rocketing the other player's ball into the woods.

1968

At the age of forty-eight, Julius Boros wins the PGA Championship, becoming the oldest player ever to gain a victory in a major. One of the game's smoothest swingers, quickest putters, and all-around fastest players, the easygoing son of Hungarian immigrants is the source of golf's most consistently ignored swing tip ("Swing easy, hit hard"), the most widely unheeded pieces of putting advice ("Miss 'em quick" and "The longer I look, the less I know"), and the least followed suggestion about pace of play ("By the time you get to your ball, if you don't know what to do with it, try another sport"). Alas, the expeditious Boros is at the twilight of his career when TV golf coverage begins in earnest, and tube-glued duffers watching televised events are now fatally influenced by the spectacle of a new generation of slow-as-molasses pros whose glacial play will inspire high handicappers who used to step right up and hit a lousy drive, a rotten second, an awful pitch, and three crummy putts without delay to take forever to hit a lousy drive, a rotten second, an awful pitch, and three crummy putts.

1969

Tony Jacklin wins the British Open, becoming the first English player in almost two decades to gain a victory in his own national championship. Later that year, he is also the beneficiary of the most remarkable—and thus far only—display of sportsmanship in Ryder Cup history when Jack Nicklaus concedes Jacklin a very missable three-foot putt to even up their match, resulting in an overall final cup score of 16–16. The generosity of the act is somewhat tempered by the fact that with the tie, the U.S. side will retain the cup, and with his characteristic eye for business opportunities, Nicklaus will ultimately find a way to cash in on his unselfish behavior when he teams up with Jacklin a few years afterward to codesign a number of golf courses whose names take prominent note of his celebrated demonstration of golfing altruism, including the Concession Golf Club, Gimme Valley, Merciful Hills, Magnanimous Heights, Charity Ridge, Gallantry Bay, Lake Grantaputt, Pickitup Point, the Links at Grand Gesture, Bigheart Creek, and Rancho Muchissimas Gracias.

1970

Doug Sanders is the innocent casualty of a rare but decisive intervention by the golfing gods at St. Andrews as they repay Nicklaus's commendable deed of the previous year by arranging matters so that Sanders's 3-foot putt on the last hole of the Old Course to win the Open drifts off to the right, forcing a play-off that he will, needless to say, lose to Nicklaus. Exhibiting a degree of remorse for which they are not usually known, the Celtic links deities—Angus Og, Blodeuwedd, Bodb, Dagda, Danu, Goibniu, Lug, Macha, and Morrigan—do their best to make it up to Sanders by seeing to it that the likable Texan, who already has a well-deserved reputation as one of the game's great money players, will never lose another golf bet as long as he lives. They also throw in that he will always get a parking space right by the clubhouse of any course he plays, and his underwear will never ride up.

"Merry Mex" Lee Trevino decides not to compete in the Masters, becoming the first active player ever to decline an invitation to the prestigious tournament. Trevino claims that he elected to skip the exclusive event because the right-to-left setup of the Augusta National golf course did not suit the open-stance, flat-swing power fade that is the key to his game, but the canny Latino reportedly later admits that the real explanation for his unprecedented demurral is that he is convinced that the only reason the redneck fat cats who run the exclusive Georgia club would send for a Mexican American is that they're looking for someone they can pay 50 cents an hour off the books to cut the grass, trim the shrubs, and repaint the Butler Cabin.

1971

In a stunning achievement that only Tiger Woods will ever come close to repeating, Lee Trevino wins the U.S., Canadian, and British Opens in a single month of spectacular play. One of the last of the legendary self-taught golfing geniuses, Trevino is among the few remaining Tour professionals who can get guidance from a swing coach, a sports psychologist, a personal trainer, and a lifestyle guru all at once, at any time of the day or night, just by talking to himself.

Apollo 14 astronaut Alan Shepard makes golf history when he uses a 6-iron clubhead mounted on the end of the handle of a soil-sample scoop to hit a golf ball on the moon. Fittingly, Shepard scores two other noteworthy firsts when he dunches his initial effort in the lunar dust with humanity's first interplanetary chili-dip and then, uttering the immortal words "Got more dirt than ball—here we go again," immediately drops another ball and wallops it "miles and miles" in mankind's inaugural extraterrestrial mulligan.

1972

Spalding introduces the Top-Flite, the first golf ball with a solid core and a nearly cut-proof synthetic cover. The cheap, durable, and reliable two-piece ball helps millions of golfers finesse the timeless dilemma posed by a forced carry over a water hazard or deep ravine. Whereas in the past, less skilled players had to choose between hitting a good shot that would fall short because they used a shit ball, or a hit a good ball that would fall short because they hit a shit shot, they can now tee up a ball that has much better odds of success even if struck poorly than a ratty old range ball or a banged-up Titleist with a big smile on one side, and if it splashes or crashes into oblivion, well, it's only a Top-Flite.

After winning the Masters and the U.S. Open in convincing fashion, Jack Nicklaus is frustrated in his effort to capture modern golf's holy grail, the single-season Grand Slam of all four major tournaments, after Lee Trevino edges him out by a single stroke at the British Open. Nicklaus's dismay is considerably intensified when, in an effort to coin a suitably memorable and headline-worthy name for his still impressive partial sweep, sportswriters come up with a number of inventive but increasingly mortifying descriptive terms, including the Hemislam, the Demislam, the Semislam, the Minislam, the Slample, the Slamella, the Slamette, the Slamicle, the Slammikin, the Slamuscule, and the Grand Slamanot.

1973

Club shafts made of graphite are marketed for the first time. The brainchild of Frank Thomas, who would go on to become technical director of the USGA, the carbon-fiber composite material dampened the joint-jarring effects of off-center impacts on the new rock-hard, two-piece balls and added some much-needed whiplike oomph to the swing speeds of soon-to-be thirty-something baby-boomer golfers. The lightweight, supple shafts were just one of a long list of '70s-era breakthrough products that have proved such a boon to the modern-day player, including Gore-Tex, Velcro, cortisone, ibuprofen, acetaminophen, and Heineken.

In what longtime golf commentator Johnny Miller will later describe as the greatest round of golf ever played, Johnny Miller shoots a record-setting final round 63 to win the U.S. Open at Oakmont in what Johnny Miller will later depict as not only the most thrilling finish in the history of the sport but also, as Johnny Miller will so memorably put it, "quite possibly the finest athletic performance of all time by a member of the human race," an achievement so awe-inspiring that years later it will move a clearly emotional Johnny Miller to tears as he remembers Johnny Miller's immortal championship performance, a demonstration of mastery of the game so complete that Johnny Miller calls it "the standard against which all future golfers for millions of years to come will be measured," a sentiment that Johnny Miller unhesitatingly endorses, portraying Johnny Miller's unforgettable victory as "quite frankly, the stuff of legend"—a legend named Johnny Miller.

1974

In the notorious "Massacre at Winged Foot," Hale Irwin hangs on to win the U.S. Open by the unheard-of score of 7 over par after the USGA, still seething over Johnny Miller's earthshaking, but infuriating, 63 at Oakmont, uses a sadistic setup to transform the already challenging

Tillinghast layout into a glorified obstacle course. The winning stroke total would have been even higher if in addition to narrowing the fairways, growing the rough, and speeding up the putting surfaces to a ridiculous degree, the demented fuddy-duddies who run the organization had adhered to their original plan to place garrulous parrots in cages on every tee to distract the pros in their backswings; put crabs in the bunkers, snakes in the hazards, and bees in the trees; and recruit eighteen retired NHL goalies to further defend par by taking up position in front of the pins and deflecting approach shots from the holes with their gloves, pads, and hockey sticks.

Alvin Clarence Thomas, better known as "Titanic Thompson," the most creative and prolific high-stakes golf hustler of all time, dies in Dallas, Texas, at the age of eighty-two. A caddie is sent out to the back nine of a local course to pass on the sad news to a foursome of golfers who often played with Titanic, though rarely for money. After a moment of silence, one of the group remarks, "I bet he isn't really dead." No one takes the wager.

1975

Lee Elder becomes the first African-American golfer to compete in the Masters, but racial progress is painfully slow in the Old South, and although Augusta National has finally hosted a black golfer, it will be another full decade before it hires its first white caddie.

Lee Trevino is struck by lightning while playing in the Western Open at Butler National, in Chicago. Trevino survives the scary mishap, later famously joking that the next time he hears thunder on a golf course, he will hold up a 1-iron since "not even God can hit a 1-iron." Trevino is mistaken. Later in the year, on the tee of the 205-yard, par-3 12th hole with a long carry over Beulah Lake at Heavenly Hills C.C. during a friendly match with Arnold Palmer, the Supreme Being shakes off the new Cobra "Baffler" 23-degree 7-wood proferred by His longtime caddie, "Angel" Gabriel, takes out His 1-iron, and knocks His ball stiff. The King wisely concedes the King of King's 6-foot putt on the spot, sparing the Holy Ghost the bother of having to summon up a providential wind gust to blow the Almighty's ball into the hole for the deuce.

1976

Utilizing a recently perfected mechanical ball-striking device called Iron Byron because it duplicates Byron Nelson's powerful but rhythmic golf swing, the USGA imposes an Overall Distance Standard for golf balls, setting an upper limit for drives of no more than 280 yards. At the same time, the game's hairsplitting rules-making body also employs a second test robot, a deliberately maladroit automaton dubbed Iron Moron that mimics the low-speed, body-heaving, reverse-pivot motion of high handicappers to establish a separate category of restrictions on the maximum length of tee shots hit by typical players, including the skied ball (70 yards), the banana ball (115 yards), the snap hook (95 yards), the cold top (60 yards), and the shank (165 yards).

1977

Al Geiberger becomes the first player to ever break 60 in a PGA tournament when he cards a bogey-free round of 59 with six pars, eleven birdies, and an eagle. His fellow professionals are both profoundly impressed by his unprecedented accomplishment and enormously relieved that it took place at the relatively minor Danny Thomas Memphis Classic rather than the U.S. Open, because otherwise they know full well that the USGA would have seen to it that next year's national championship was held on a par-52 course with two-yard-wide fairways lined with corn mazes and the holes cut horizontally in the sides of the collection areas surrounding the greens.

In a bizarre incident that adds an unexpected element of suspense to an already rousing finale, Hubert Green is quietly informed during the last round of the U.S. Open at Southern Hills that he is the target of a death threat. The shaken but steadfast Green soldiers on to win the tournament by a single stroke and no attempt is ever made on his life, but the freakish event has a lasting impact on the game when the PGA, with its well-honed commercial instincts, seeks to exploit the sense of high drama conjured up during the last minutes of the Open by instituting a sudden-death play-off format for the first time in that year's PGA Championship at Pebble Beach. Taste does, however, prevail over showmanship as the PGA abandons its original scheme of having a tournament official dressed up as the Grim Reaper complete with hooded cloak, hourglass, and scythe accompany Lanny Wadkins and Gene Littler during their tie-breaking showdown, cutting away repeatedly to a live shot of a stonemason standing ready to chisel the name of the defeated competitor into a consolation-prize tombstone, and positioning a hearse next to the trophy platform to convey the loser to the parking lot.

Tom Watson dispels a reputation as a player who can't seem to quite close the deal by winning both the Masters and the British Open, defeating longtime rival Jack Nicklaus in a pair of down-to-the-wire cliffhangers. Although both contests are at the top of the list of all-time head-to-head matchups, arguably the most unforgettable is the renowned Duel in the Sun at the Ailsa links in Turnberry, which is famed not just for the tremendous emotion of the heart-stopping back-and-forth competitive play during the final round of the battle royal between the two golfing titans, but also for the truly astounding fact, given the typical summer weather in northern Scotland, that it is not known as Duel in the Drizzle, Duel in the Shower, Duel in the Drencher, Duel in the Soaker, Duel in the Squall, Duel in the Rainstorm, Duel in the Cloudburst, Duel in the Downpour, Duel in the Deluge, or Duel in the Monsoon.

1978

In one of the more remarkable debuts on the women's golf tour, Nancy Lopez wins nine tournaments, five of which were consecutive, during her first full year as an LPGA professional. As a young girl, Lopez lived in Roswell, New Mexico, site of the famous UFO incident, and played at a local 9-hole course where she was mentored by Klovdob 8 MuxNyp, a marooned flying-saucer-crash survivor who was using the skills he acquired as an amateur xarff champion back home on the planet Sneelg to eke out a living as a golf pro. The small-statured, green-complectioned starship pilot, who passed himself off as a Scottish midget with a skin condition, taught Lopez the signature looping swing with a slow takeaway he learned on his low-gravity home world, which she used to such good effect to capture a career total of forty-eight tour victories, though she never could master telekinetic putting or the fourteen-finger Zargon grip.

1979

Unable on such short notice to obtain a tall enough plastic windmill with rotating blades or a large enough rubber dinosaur, the USGA plants a tree overnight to block the shortcut on a dogleg hole taken by several players during the first round of the U.S. Open at Inverness Club in Toledo, Ohio.

TaylorMade introduces the first metal woods. Resilient, durable, and easy to hit, the new clubs are an instant success, but they do pose an odd little problem, particularly for TV sports commentators, as the only names anyone can think up to call the things—fairway metals, the 3-metal, the 5-metal, the utility metal—sound so dopey. On the other hand, the rapid adoption of the new clubs by players everywhere does remove a long-standing source of confusion in the game, since from now on the term "the woods" will no longer be employed to describe the more or less bulb-shaped, round-backed, flat-soled clubs used to hit balls long distances, but will be used exclusively to refer to the balls' most frequent destination.

A brash and dazzling young Spanish golfer named Severiano Ballesteros captures the British Open—and the hearts of the normally xenophobic English fans—with his bold, flamboyant play, typified by an incredible recovery shot he made from a parking lot to birdie the 16th hole in the final round at Royal Lytham & St. Annes. The first player from continental Europe to win the Open in more than seven decades, Seve's instant popularity is due to a number of unique qualities much appreciated by the Brits: He is fiercely competitive, he is not an American, he is a risk taker and a shot maker, he is not an American, he is emotional and exciting to watch, he is not an American, his game epitomizes touch and feel, he is not an American, he is colorful and charming, and, to top it all off, he is not an American.

1980

The PGA inaugurates the Senior Tour, later known as the Champions Tour. Although it was conceived primarily as a long-overdue payday for the generation of professionals who missed out on the gargantuan purses of the modern era, the Tour, with its calendar of no-cut, three-round birdie fests on a rota of short, friendly courses, provides something of genuine, if intangible, value to legions of moderately skilled fifty-something club players as well. From now on, a onetime club champion with a single-digit handicap can muse out loud about his determination to take some lessons, practice hard, and sharpen up his game for a possible run as a senior pro and simply be dismissed as harmlessly delusional, whereas previously, any amateur, no matter how skilled, who voiced a similar intention about making a serious bid to qualify for the regular Tour would run the very real risk of being certified as clinically insane and immediately transported to the nearest mental institution in a heavily padded van.

The PGA Tournament Players Club, the first in a series of fan-friendly stadium courses conceived by commissioner Deane Beman, opens at Sawgrass in Florida. The Pete Dye–designed monstrosity features three grueling finishing holes, including the notorious par-3 island green 17th, which help bring to the game of golf the same high degree of keen interest among knowledgeable devotees of the sport that flame-engulfed multivehicle crashes provide for spectators at Nascar races.

1981

The USGA institutes a U.S. Mid-Amateur Championship limited to players twenty-five and older to provide first-rate recreational golfers with a venue where they can compete on an equal basis with their peers without being consistently outclassed by the latest crop of soon-to-turn-professional top college players. Concurrently, the USGA gave serious consideration to the introduction of a quartet of additional restricted-eligibility amateur events, including the U.S. Dub-Amateur, for golfers with handicaps of 20 or higher; the U.S. Dim-Amateur, for golfers with IQs of 100 or less; the U.S. Tub-Amateur, for golfers with a body mass index greater than 30; and the U.S. Sot-Amateur for golfers who on both the first tee and at the turn have a minimum blood alcohol level of 1.5, but quickly abandoned the plan after concluding that the four proposed events would be oversubscribed to such a degree as to be totally unmanageable.

Bernhard Langer, who would go on to win two Masters, becomes the first native of Germany ever to win the German Open in its entire seventy-year history. It is also the first time in recent memory that a German has received an award for shooting a total of 277 and no one had to figure out what to do with all the bodies.

1982

In the latest chapter in their ongoing rivalry, Tom Watson follows up a narrow win over Jack Nicklaus in that year's Masters with a second sweet victory, snatching yet another major from under the Golden Bear's nose by chipping in for a birdie on the 17th hole at Pebble Beach to take the trophy almost literally out of Jack's hands in the final round of the U.S. Open. A peeved Nicklaus responds by hiring a couple of valet parkers from the Lodge at Pebble Beach to fill Watson's tournament courtesy car with range balls, and Watson immediately retaliates by arranging to have the air let out of the tires of Jack's corporate jet at Monterey Airport and seeing to it that a set of drawings for his latest golf course design is replaced with blueprints for a sewage treatment plant.

Seven-time PGA Tour winner Jerry Pate dumps two real stinkers into a water hazard on the final hole of the new TPC course at Sawgrass when, after clinching his victory in the inaugural Players Championship, he throws PGA commissioner Deane Beman and course architect Pete Dye into the lake beside the 18th green.

1983

The PGA Tour adopts a new policy doubling the number of players exempt from weekly pretournament qualifying rounds from the top 60 on the money list to the top 125 and setting the cutoff point for required attendance at the annual Q-School at 126 on the list and above. Although this is a welcome development for the surprisingly large number of touring pros who are playing week in and week out for a regular paycheck rather than a bulging trophy case, it does inevitably create a situation some years hence when a record 2,478 singularly unrenowned players will have been voted into the World Golf Hall of Obscurity at Lake Nepenthe in Florida, as opposed to the approximately 130 who have been inducted into its somewhat more prestigious sister organization, the World Golf Hall of Fame in St. Augustine. To qualify for consideration on the ballot as a Hall of No Famer, candidates must have failed to distinguish themselves in one or more of four key categories of nonperformance: (1) a member of the PGA or LPGA Tour who is at least forty years old, has been on the Tour for ten years, has won no major tournaments and no more than one regular Tour event, or a member of the Champions Tour who has managed to remain winless for at least five years; (2) an international player who has preserved a victory-free record in Europe, Asia, and Australia; (3) a veteran whose totally forgettable career concluded at least thirty years earlier and who demonstrated an ability to make a comfortable living without accomplishing anything of note in the annals of competitive play; or (4) an individual with a history of lifetime nonachievement in the sport, who has consistently displayed a conspicuous lack of any discernible contribution whatsoever to the game of golf.

1984

Golf instruction videotapes are widely marketed for the first time, but for some years to come, duct tape will remain the gold standard for swing fixes.

The Jack Nicklaus–designed Desert Highlands golf course opens in Scottsdale, Arizona. It is the earliest example of the "geriatric school" of golf architecture, a new breed of condo-lined, cactus-dotted Sun Belt retirement community layouts that feature compact, slice-friendly, overwatered pipeline fairways, cart paths with passing lanes and guardrails, pressure-activated "talking" yardage markers, bathrooms on all the par-5s and long par 4s, and combination ball washer–defibrillator units on every tee.

1985

Bolstered by the solid play of the new Spanish contingent led by Seve Ballesteros, the recently expanded British-Irish-European side wins the Ryder Cup for the first time in almost a quarter of a century. Stung by the loss, the Americans vow to revamp their entire playing strategy, opting for spiffier team uniforms from higher-end designers, persuading the players' wives to use more lip gloss and less eyeliner, and introducing a considerably expanded range of Ryder Cup logo merchandise at a wider variety of price points.

The USGA introduces the Slope System, which assigns golf courses a number from 55 to 155 based on their comparative degrees of difficulty in order to permit appropriate adjustments in the handicaps of golfers. The course rating index takes into account, among other things, Topography (uphill, downhill, and sidehill lies), Rough (extent and density), Fairways (width and length), Bunkers (placement and severity), Hazards (size and the presence of any forced carries over them), and Greens (speed and the trickiness of the hole locations), but, incredibly, it omits the four categories of playability of the greatest importance to golfers: Refreshments (accessibility and affordability of properly chilled adult beverages), Shrubbery (prevalence of heavily vegetated areas suitable for use as an impromptu sanitary facility), Range Balls (quality and availability for theft for later use in challenging shots), and Vigilance (relative feasibility of sneaking onto a public course without paying or a private one as a nonmember).

1986

Greg Norman, the incomparably talented but perpetually snakebitten Australian with movie-star looks and awesome ball-striking skills, gains the dubious distinction of being the first player to achieve the "Saturday Slam," by holding the lead going into the final round of all four majors but managing to win only the British Open, which he got around to blowing on another occasion with a last-minute meltdown at Troon. Ten years later, his agonizing collapse at the 1996 Masters led to a crushing loss to Nick Faldo, but "the Shark" saved the most memorable stumble of all for last when, on March 15, 1997, President Bill Clinton fell down the stairs at Norman's Hobe Sound home, injuring his knee badly enough to require surgery.

At the age of forty-six, Jack Nicklaus wins his sixth green jacket and completes a quartet of career slams in one of the most riveting performances in sports history. Two months later, forty-three-year-old Raymond Floyd takes the U.S. Open trophy at Shinnecock. The two late-season triumphs clearly demonstrate that although it is an accepted piece of golfing wisdom that competing professionally at the highest levels has become a young man's game, that maxim does not hold true if the young man in question is Greg Norman.

Easy-on-the-eye Australian sex symbol Jan Stephenson, who won more than a dozen LPGA events, including three majors, appears in a photograph reclining naked in a bathtub full of strategically positioned golf balls and later poses for a pinup calendar, earning her the Association of Golf Sportswriters' title as Nookie of the Year.

1987

Craig Stadler is penalized two strokes during the San Diego Open for "building a stance" by using a towel to kneel on to play a scrambling shot, then is disqualified for signing an incorrect scorecard. The Walrus escapes a far more serious penalty, however, when owing to his considerable bulk, the beefy, hot-tempered Stadler is unable to catch the USGA rules official he chased across the clubhouse parking lot whom he reportedly planned to slay and eat.

The European team inflicts a particularly humiliating defeat on the U.S. side in the Ryder Cup on their home turf, vanquishing a squad captained by Jack Nicklaus in a rout at Muirfield Village, a course he helped design. Stunned by their second consecutive humbling at the hands of the Euros, the American golfers decide to turn up the heat, vowing to be better prepared next time with many additional items of patriotic gear, including Star-Spangled Banner cell phone ring tones and sets of Mt. Rushmore–style presidential clubhead covers; much more stylish hairdos for the players' wives, including up-sweeps, bouffants, feather cuts, and swirled and layered looks; and larger, heavier, and more expensive Rolex wristwatches for every member of the team.

After spending two years working with legendary golf teacher David Leadbetter to rebuild the inconsistent golf swing that let him down all too often when the heat was on, earning him the unflattering nickname "Nick Fold-o," Nick Faldo returns to competitive play and promptly wins the British Open with a convincing display of methodical robogolf that featured a final round during which he carded eighteen straight pars. Twenty years later, with an impressive record of six majors under his belt, but also burdened with an unfortunate reputation as a cold, remote, self-centered sourpuss that gained him the new nickname, "Nick the Prick," Faldo turns to another coach, the mysterious golf psychiatrist Dr. Simon Headbender, to reshape his psyche. Not long afterward, he emerges as the most charming, engaging, witty, insightful, and popular commentator in the history of TV golf coverage, with the considerably more satisfying nickname of "Nick, the Incredibly Highly Paid Sports Personality Who Gets to Trade Quips with Killer Cutie Kelly Tilghman and Have His Butt Nuzzled by Big-League Brownnose Jim Nantz."

1988

Curtis Strange wins the first of two consecutive U.S. Opens. His successful defense of the title the following year would mark the first time any player had captured the trophy twice in a row since Ben Hogan's storied back-to-back wins in 1950 and 1951. Much impressed with his own feat, Strange exuberantly exclaimed, "Move over, Ben Hogan," to which the Hawk responded with the tart and astute riposte, "Make room, Jack Fleck." Strange never won again on the Tour.

Ignoring the trivial threats to the integrity of the game posed by several looming innovations like the long-shafted split-grip putter, the oversized titanium-headed Big Bertha driver, and golf balls that are clearly capable of being hit well over 350 yards, the USGA decides to ban as nonconforming the grooves on the clubfaces of Ping Eye 2 Irons.

1989

Four golfers score holes in one on the par-3 6th hole at Oak Hill on the same day during the U.S. Open. The USGA toys with the idea of placing the pin in an active sprinkler head for the following round but reluctantly decides that the resultant intermittent wetting of the nearly dead bent grass on the putting surface will only serve to allow players who land their tee shots on the laughably fast green but who do not make an ace to somehow still rescue a par.

Having failed to realize that in Ping founder and owner Karsten Solheim they have, amazingly enough, encountered an individual as obstinate, arrogant, conceited, and boneheaded as they are, the governing board of the

USGA quietly settles the lawsuit he brought against the organization, modifying the iron-groove ban to grandfather in the original clubs and apply the new regulations only to future models. Chastened, they turn their attention to more pressing issues, legalizing hollowheaded plastic bunker rakes, setting a maximum amount of cleaning fluid in ball washers at one gallon (3.78 liters), and establishing an overall standard diameter of 3 inches (76.2 mm) for golf cart cup holders.

1990

Following a controversy during the PGA Championship at the Shoal Creek Golf Club in Birmingham, Alabama, the PGA announces that it will no longer hold tournaments at golf clubs that do not have at least one African-American and one woman member. Seeking to close a pair of potential loopholes, the PGA further stipulates that the African-American member must not have been deceased at the time of his election, no matter how recent his demise, and the woman member must not be inflatable.

Belatedly bowing to the inevitable, the R&A agrees to adopt as a worldwide standard the USGA's specification of 1.68" for the diameter of the golf ball but retains the British guideline of no more than 3½ hours for the time allotted for the completion by a four-ball match of a competitive 18-hole round of golf, as opposed to the American norm of 5¼ hours, and preserves the local custom of expressing disdain to a fellow player by pumping the right arm in a vigorous upward motion of the fist with the left hand held in the crook of the right elbow, rather than simply extending the middle finger of the right hand.

Fresh from his costly Pyrrhic victory over the USGA in the groove wars, Karsten Solheim and his wife, Louise, establish the Solheim Cup, a Ryder Cup–style competition designed to contribute to the cause of gender equity in golf by providing an equal opportunity for leading American and European lady professionals to engage in the kind of rotten, ugly, boorish, shabby, and unsportspersonlike behavior in an international match play event that had up until now been the sole prerogative of the premier male golfers.

The Ben Hogan Tour is created as a minor-league feeder system for the PGA Tour. It will later be known as the Nike Tour, the Buy.com Tour, the Nationwide Tour, and the United States Treasury Troubled Asset Relief Program Multibillion-dollar Bank Bailout Tour.

1991

Added to the field at the last moment when Nick Price unexpectedly withdraws, the ninth alternate, an unheralded rookie named John Daly, wins the PGA Tournament at Crooked Stick with an unparalleled display of ball-striking power and putting magic that makes him an instant and lasting crowd favorite. A true original who breaks the mold of the lean, bland, clean-living clones who dominate the modern Tour, Daly not only drives the ball farther and putts better than they do, he also smokes, drinks, gambles, and has marital troubles, which make his enormous appeal to regular duffers no mystery, since although none of them has his prodigious length off the tee or his deft short game touch, many of them have mastered most, if not all, of the other four key elements of his distinctive golfing persona.

Ian Woosnam, the bantam golf sensation from Wales, wins the Masters. Caught off guard by Woosie's out-of-nowhere victory, Augusta Chairman Jack Stephens toys with the idea of Welshproofing the course by planting plump and tasty-looking leeks in the rough and filling the bunkers with a savory melted cheese concoction, but after consulting an atlas in the club's vast, five-volume library and discovering that Wales is not, as he had thought, a populous state in the golfing powerhouse nation of Australia, but rather a tiny principality on the west coast of England, he concludes that the odds of a future conquest by hordes of Cumbrian golfers are slim.

Phil Mickelson wins the Northern Telecom Tucson Open at age twenty, becoming the last amateur player thus far to achieve a victory in a regular PGA Tour event. A natural right-hander playing golf against his dominant side, Mickelson would appear to have created for himself an unnecessary obstacle to mastery of an already challenging game by adopting the seemingly unnatural southpaw setup, but this counterintuitive approach proves to be both an effective ball-striking method and a shrewd career strategy for the agreeable but streaky and often headstrong player who, in spite of a somewhat spotty record, will nevertheless manage, with relatively little effort, to instantly vault to the top of the list of the greatest left-handed players of all time.

On the 18th hole of the final match of the Ryder Cup at Kiawah Island, Bernhard Langer misses a 7-foot putt to hand a narrow victory to the U.S. side in the aptly named "War on the Shore." Langer is devastated by the defeat, but, really, he should have remembered that Germans tend to lose these war things, and anyway, on the bright side, his yipped knee-knocker was nowhere near as mortifying as Hitler's notorious two shots in the bunker in Berlin in 1945.

1992

At the age of forty-nine, and almost three decades after his first career Tour victory, Raymond Floyd wins the Doral Open and quickly secures product endorsement contracts to wear the logos of Geritol, Polygrip, and Preparation H on his hats and shirts.

Fred Couples wins the Masters when he catches an unbelievable break as his drive on the par-3 12th hole in Augusta's treacherous Amen Corner comes up short yet somehow manages to cling to a tiny clump of grass on the closely mown slope below the hole instead of rolling back down into Rae's Creek. Even though everyone agrees that the amazing stroke of good fortune could not possibly have happened to a nicer guy, Club Chairman Jack Stephens immediately lays plans to replant the bank the following year with specially bred, hand-seeded, superslick, ultraflat-lying, guaranteed fluke-free, 99.97 percent luckless, one-leafed clover.

IV

HOLING OUT
1993–2009

1993

Golf prodigy Tiger Woods wins an unprecedented third consecutive U.S. Junior Amateur, capping his perfect record of prior victories in a series of competitive events for younger players, including the U.S. Preschool Amateur, the U.S. Toddler Amateur, the U.S. Infant Amateur, the U.S. Newborn Amateur, the U.S. Fetus Amateur, and the U.S. Embryo Amateur.

Nick Price sets a new annual earnings record, taking home just under $1.5 million in prize money. A citizen of Zimbabwe who later moved to Florida, Price's tour winnings would have been worth $65 million billion in his home country's wildly inflated currency, allowing him, on paper at least, to edge out Tiger Woods for the title of the golfing world's first quadrillionaire.

Softspikes are introduced and quickly made mandatory at most golf courses. Their advent is a godsend to greenkeepers, but the disappearance of the old metal spikes and the silencing of their happy clatter on parking lot pavements, together with the simultaneous shift from the tradition of golfers walking the course to a near-universal reliance on motorized golf carts by players of all ages, eliminates once and for all the pretense that golf is an actual sport, like tennis, rather than a time-killing pastime, like shopping.

1994

In what legendary golf champion–turned–TV commentator Johnny Miller would subsequently portray as one of the most extraordinary, astounding, electrifying, earthshaking, breathtaking, magical, synonym-depleting, out-of-the-blue returns to tip-top golfing form ever recorded in the annals of Western civilization, an achievement that in ancient times would have been solemnly depicted in fancy bas-reliefs incised into the walls of imposing temples and other architecturally significant structures, and jubilantly celebrated in song and verse by wild-eyed, ill-shaven wandering bards, legendary golf champion–turned–TV commentator Johnny Miller comes out of retirement to win the AT&T National Pro-Am at Pebble Beach, an accomplishment that Miller himself is forced

to concede represents a milestone in the sport so dumb-
founding that it instantly transforms the rest of the upcoming golfing year's results into mere footnotes to the
latest and most momentous chapter in the astounding
history of the man called Johnny Miller.

In mere footnotes to Johnny Miller's sensational season-
opening performance, José María Olazabal becomes the
second Spaniard and the seventh non-American to win
the Masters, South African Ernie Els becomes the second South African to win the U.S. Open, Nick Price
wins both the British Open and the PGA Tournament,

Greg Norman sets a new course record at Sawgrass to win the Tournament Players Championship and, at age eighteen, Tiger Woods becomes the youngest man ever to win the U.S. Amateur, the first of his unprecedented string of three consecutive victories in the event.

Natural Golf promotes a revolutionary new method of play based on the unorthodox and strikingly simple single-plane swing of Moe Norman, the shy, eccentric Ontario native who many students of the game believe was the greatest ball striker of all time. Videos of Moe employing his idiosyncratic short takeaway and abbreviated follow-through to hit the amazingly accurate and consistent shots that were his trademark give rise to the troubling, but for many hackers the strangely satisfying, suspicion that virtually every single thing that anyone has ever said, written, or taught about the golf swing may turn out to be totally and completely wrong.

1995

After serving as a pallbearer earlier that week at the funeral of his longtime teacher and mentor Harvey Penick Jr., Ben Crenshaw dissolves in tears on the 18th green at Augusta as he wins his second Masters at the age of forty-three. It's an equally emotional moment for the publishers of Penick's all-time bestselling golf memoir-cum-manual, *The Little Red Book*, and its feeble but lucrative spinoffs, *For All Who Love the Game*, *The Game for a Lifetime*, and *If You Play Golf, You're My Friend*, who now have to pull the plug on a planned rollout of another pair of cheesy sequels, *There's a Golfer Born Every Minute*, and *My Desk Is a Mess but I Know There's Another Golf Book Here Somewhere*.

When commentator Gary McCord remarks during the on-air coverage of the Masters that the 17th green is so fast it must have been "bikini-waxed," the stuffy tournament hosts bristle at the use of such coarse language to describe their hallowed venue and demand that CBS drop the wisecracking analyst from its future broadcasts at Augusta. Fearful of losing their rights to televise the prestigious and highly profitable championship, the network instantly knuckles under and gives McCord the boot, which emboldens the club hierarchy to take matters one step farther and insist on other forms of approved terminology. From now on, in addition to the requirement that the spectators be referred to not as "fans" or "crowds" but rather as "patrons"; the "patrons" are to be depicted not as "drunk" but instead described as "bibulous" or "over-served"; the greens have not been "speeded up," they were "accelerated," "expedited," or "alacritized"; the course has not been "lengthened," it has been "augmented" or "en-hanced"; there is no "rough" on any of the holes, though some of the grass on the edges of the fairways is "lush," "luxuriant," or, in a few cases, even "exuberant"; there are no "rain delays," only "precipitational pauses" and "meteorological hiatuses"; players do not "choke," they "blench," "misgive," or "become discommoded"; they do not "blow" their chances, they "lapse" or "retrogress"; and the Masters is never won by a "long shot" or a "dark horse," although from time to time an "unrecognized prospect" or an "unheralded contender" may gain the green jacket. The humbled TV executives take revenge by doubling the number of times they play the warbly, turgid signature tune that brackets every segment of their coverage and that is generally regarded as the single worst piece of music ever composed for a sporting event, with the possible exception of the migraine-triggering theme from the Sylvester Stallone *Rocky* movies.

A century after the second official U.S. Open was held at Shinnecock Hills in Southampton, Corey Pavin wins the centennial edition of the event, hitting a flawless 4-wood approach shot stiff to the pin on the 18th hole of the final round at the venerable seaside links course. Much has changed in the game in the intervening hundred years, including the amount of the winner's purse, which has ballooned from $150 to $350,000; the size of the crowds, which have grown from a few hundred spectators to thirty thousand; and the average length of a drive, which has increased from a little over 200 yards to just under 300; but the merchandise tent is still filled with overpriced sleazy crap, the beer still tastes like something died in it, and even though the onlookers' shouts have been shortened from "You, sir, are indeed the man of the hour!" to "You da man!" the galleries are still packed with the kind of jerks you get paired with at pricey resorts in a six-hour round from hell.

Smooth-swinging Australian pro Steve Elkington temporarily overcomes a crippling sinus condition that burdened him with one of the most implausible and debilitating disabilities in the history of the game—a severe allergy to grass. Other players in more recent times who have struggled with similarly incapacitating conditions include Payne Stewart, who was allergic to tasteful golfing attire, Colin Montgomerie, who is allergic to Americans, and Jean Van de Velde, who is allergic to himself.

In the single most demanding and out-of-character divine intervention in his nearly two-millennium-long career as a beatified being, St. Andrew sees to it that, regardless of its source, ingredients, or prior alcoholic content, every beverage that approaches John Daly's lips will be instantly transformed into Diet Coke, and a stone-cold-sober J.D. wins the British Open at the namesake course of the Scottish nation's sanctified, venerated, revered, and now very strung-out spiritual patron.

After considering, and then rejecting, several possible cable-TV network formats, including the Beer Channel, the Snack Channel, and the Nap Channel, media entrepreneur Joe Gibbs finally settles on a winning concept that successfully embraces the critical audience-attracting attributes of all three and founds the hugely profitable Golf Channel.

The World Cup of Golf is held at Mission Hills in Shen-zhen, becoming the first international golf championship to take place in China. It is also the first golf tournament openly sponsored by manufacturers of knockoff golf equipment, including Pong, Coalaway, Cleeveling, Taylow-Make, Nikey, Toottleist, Cobla, Sunny Mountains, Adodahs, and Joyful Foot.

Several months after golf analyst Ben Wright makes a number of offensive comments about the LPGA Tour, including the observation that "women are handicapped by having boobs," he is finally fired by CBS Sports, which evidently came to the belated conclusion that TV networks are also handicapped by having boobs.

1996

Star-crossed former world number-one player Greg Norman shoots a horrifying final round 78 at Augusta, squandering a 5-shot lead and losing the Masters to Nick Faldo to close out his golfing career just a single fizzle away from bringing off a second lifetime Grand Slump sweep of runner-up finishes in major championships.

After taking his third and final U.S. Amateur title, Tiger Woods turns pro, wins two of the five events he enters, makes it into the top thirty on the annual money list in just a few brief months of play, and is named the PGA Tour Rookie of the Year, the Decade, the Century, and the Millennium.

Annika Sorenstam wins her second consecutive U.S. Women's Open, which stands as the most significant episode in Swedish golfing history until some five years later when her compatriot Jesper Parnevik introduces Tiger Woods to his au pair, Scandinavian fashion-magazine bombshell Elin Nordegren.

1997

Tiger Woods becomes the youngest player in history to win the Masters, dominating Augusta National with a record-setting 18-under-par 72-hole final score of 270 that gave him an unheard-of 12-stroke victory margin. The mesmerizing display of power, shot-making skill, and nerveless putting by the sensational new superstar prompts erstwhile golfing wunderkind Jack Nicklaus to observe that Woods is now playing a game that *he* is not familiar with, and inspires wisecracking 1979 Masters winner Fuzzy Zoeller to take note of Tiger's achievement by remarking to a group of reporters, "That little boy is driving well and he's putting well," and suggesting that at next year's past champions dinner when Tiger gets to choose the menu they "tell him not to serve fried chicken or collard greens or whatever the hell they serve." Zoeller quickly offers Woods an apology for the comments, which Tiger accepts, but the perception of racism costs Fuzzy over $1 million in withdrawn sponsorship deals, a painful reminder that of all of the pernicious faults and flaws that even top professional players can fall victim to—the flying elbow, the locked knees, the lifted shoulder, and the swaying hip—by far the most damaging is the foot in the mouth.

Ernie Els, the laid-back, even-demeanored South African with a smooth-as-silk, unhurried playing tempo, wins his second U.S. Open. Hackers everywhere dream of emulating the Big Easy's relaxed, perfectly paced, athletic ball-striking motion, but sadly, if they do somehow manage to copy his leisurely, seemingly effortless swing, their shots only go about thirty-five yards.

As Davis Love III takes his victory stroll up the 18th fairway at Winged Foot on his way to claiming the PGA Championship's prestigious Wanamaker Trophy, a timely rainbow obligingly spans the sky, providing a nice accompaniment to the ho-hum, run-of-the-mill pots of gold Tour players typically encounter at the conclusion of golf tournaments.

Acknowledging the critical contribution of the Spanish contingent of golfers to the revival of the formerly lopsided competition, the Ryder Cup is held for the first time at a course in continental Europe, the Valderrama Golf Club on the Costa del Sol. European Captain Seve Ballesteros leads his squad to a narrow, hard-fought victory amid protests from the American side over Seve's out-of-control gamesmanship, but the passionate and enthusiastic Iberian crowds bring a welcome energy to the proceedings with their lusty huzzahs and high-spirited plaudits, and players on both teams who hail from predominantly English-speaking countries have the opportunity to enrich their vocabularies with colorful local expressions of support and encouragement including *¡cabrón!* ("well done!"), *¡hijo de puta!* ("heck of a putt!"), *¡chinga tu madre!* ("you are the man!"), *¡besame el culo!* ("take a bow!"), *¡maricon!* ("jolly good!"), *¡come mierda!* ("marvelous shot!"), *¡chupa mi pinga!* ("your play amazes me!"), and *¡ay pendejo!* ("you were robbed!").

1998

Raising the intriguing possibility that Tiger Woods's magic is so intense that it may actually rub off on someone he plays with frequently, his close friend, neighbor, and regular off-season golfing companion Mark O'Meara wins both the Masters and the British Open at the age of forty-one, in spite of the challenges posed by the superstition-driven but, in retrospect, entirely rational decision he made following his final late-winter friendly round with Woods not to bathe or change his clothes for the remainder of the year.

Handicapped professional Casey Martin, who suffers from a birth defect that makes it difficult and painful for him to walk more than a short distance, is permitted by the USGA to use a cart at the U.S. Open, but he has to sue the PGA under the Americans with Disabilities Act to obtain a similar exemption for the Tour. Martin's position is strongly endorsed and advocated by adherents of the new movement for political correctness whose influence on golf is symbolized by the annual P. C. Open Tournapeoplet at the Sustainable Hills Golf Cooperative's 5,600-yard, par-92, award-sharing course in Santa Cruz, California, an organic, low-spray, bias-free, gender-neutral, culturally sensitive layout with no hazards, bunkers, or rough, no forced carries, and no optically challenged holes (formerly known as "blind shots"). Needless to say, there is no cut in the event, the winner is the player with the least worst score, and everyone in the field gets his or her name on the trophy.

1999

When Tiger's ball ends up stymied behind an enormous rock at the Phoenix Open, two dozen fans step up and roll the half-ton boulder out of the way, allowing Woods to go for the green instead of having to chip out sideways into the fairway. Although there is some question whether the outside interference is permissible, rules officials quickly sanction the action, determining that the massive piece of rubble is a Loose Monolith and hence may be removed without penalty. They also rely on some other obscure but potent stipulations buried in footnotes in the Decisions and Decrees of the USGA, including Due Deference to a Person of Note or Consequence, Legitimacy of Actions Taken by an Indispensable Object of Media Attention, and Recognition of the Key Role Played by the Only Golfer Anyone Gives a Shit About in This Whole Stupid Tournament.

In the zaniest display of sheer, unadulterated numskullery in the annals of a sport that is not exactly lacking in instances of deeply stupid behavior, the then little-known but soon never-to-be-forgotten French pro Jean Van de Velde makes a monumental bouillabaisse of the final hole at Carnoustie, hitting a series of the most stupefyingly knuckleheaded golf shots ever witnessed in a major tournament to blow a comfortable lead in the British Open with a positively thermonuclear detonation. As his caddie later explained with a typically rueful Gallic shrug, "Monsieur Jean, he is—how do you say—a few eggs short of an omelette."

Tiger Woods parts company with his caddie, Mike "Fluff" Cowan, for what are described as "undisclosed reasons," but it is widely assumed that the dismissal was triggered by an interview Fluff gave to *Golf Digest* in which he revealed details of their financial arrangements and discussed other personal matters that Woods regarded as an invasion of his carefully guarded privacy. Later that year, Woods also changed his brand of footwear after a pair of his golf shoes went on *The Oprah Winfrey Show* to promote their tell-all book, *Walking with a Tiger: In the Footsteps of Golf's Greatest Player.*

Apparently seeking to replace Fluff Cowan with someone more along the lines of Bond villain Auric Goldfinger's malevolent looper, Oddjob, Tiger Wood hires cranky knuckle-dragging Kiwi goon, Steve Williams, who soon gains distinction as the only professional PGA Tour caddie to use his game management skills to club both his player and the spectators.

After Justin Leonard sinks a gargantuan 45-footer on the 17th hole of the final match of the Ryder Cup at The Country Club in Brookline, Massachusetts, the American players and their wives prance around the green in a tasteless celebration of what they accurately foresee as their amazing comeback victory, in spite of the fact that José María Olazabal has yet to attempt, and predictably miss, his own long putt. The inexcusable display of discourtesy and bad manners leads to calls on both sides of the Atlantic for the organizers of the biennial international competition to abandon the fiction that the event is a gentlemanly sporting encounter, and replace the current tournament format of alternate-shot, better-ball, and singles golf matches with a food fight, a paint-ball war, and a knock-down, drag-out, no-holds-barred demolition derby using souped-up gas-powered golf carts with battering rams welded to their bumpers.

2000

Fijian Vijay Singh wins the Masters, becoming the first citizen of an oddball, out-of-the-golfing-limelight country to don the green jacket in the twenty-first century, a distinction he will share three years later with Canadian

Mike Weir. While Singh's and Weir's victories at Augusta are above all testaments to the tireless work ethic they both share, the twin successes of the unlikely duo do raise the question of how Fiji, a tiny, impoverished Pacific island republic with just over 800,000 inhabitants, and Canada, a vast, wealthy, continent-spanning nation with a population of 33,000,000, ended up producing the same number of top golfers—one.

Tiger Woods breezes to victory in the U.S. Open at Pebble Beach with a score of 12 under par, runs away with the British Open at St. Andrews with a 19-under-par round, and prevails in the PGA Championship at Valhalla in a play-off after finishing in regulation play with an 18-under-par total that featured seven birdies in the last twelve holes. Woods also won eight of the other twenty-one tournaments he entered during the year, including the Canadian Open, which made him the only player other than Lee Trevino to claim the "Triple Crown" single-year sweep of the U.S., British, and Canadian Opens, and his season scoring average of 68.17 bested what was long thought to be the unbeatable record of 68.33 set in 1945 by Byron Nelson. Following this triumphant procession of championship romps, the PGA Tour

gave serious consideration to renaming itself the Tiger Tour, replacing its trademark logo depicting a golfer at the finish of his backswing with an image of a golfer executing a fist pump, and changing its slogan from "These guys are good" to "This guy is really, really, really good."

2001

Tiger Woods, who at the age of twenty-four had already become the youngest player ever to achieve the career Slam of majors with his previous year's victory at the U.S. Open, wins his second Masters and completes the "Tiger Slam," becoming the first player in history to hold all four of the top professional tournament trophies simultaneously. His lead in the international golf rankings at this point is so huge that he could have taken all of 2001 off and still have been the World #1 player, which suggests that he is not only one of the greatest golfers of all time, he is probably at least three of the greatest golfers of all time, and is very likely to end up being as many as five of the greatest golfers of all time.

After hiring washed-up Belgian rock star–turned–wacko golf guru Jos Vanstiphout to give him a confidence boost, mild-mannered South African Retief Goosen prevails in an 18-hole Monday play-off to win the first of his two U.S. Open titles, demonstrating yet again that the game of golf is 90 percent mental and 10 percent mental.

David Duval, who a couple of years earlier had taken the Tour and Players Championship titles, had twice been runner-up in the Masters, and had won the Bob Hope Desert Classic with a final-round 59, coasts to victory in the British Open, but his game suddenly and mysteriously deserts him, and he soon earns the unwelcome distinction of being the only one of the many millions of golfers in the world who can't break 80 who once broke 60.

2002

Tiger Woods outlasts Phil Mickelson to win the U.S. Open at New York State's Bethpage Black course, carding the only subpar round in the tournament. It is the first time the USGA has staged the national championship at a publicly owned facility, signaling a potentially tectonic shift in the organization's choice of playing venues away from golf courses where you can only get a tee time if you're a millionaire or know a member to golf courses where you can only get a tee time if you're a demon speed-dialer or know the governor.

2003

Martha Burk, chairperson of the National Council of Women's Organizations, stages a demonstration against Augusta National's status as a men-only club. Her protest gains comparatively little traction, but it does provoke club Chairman Hootie Johnson to issue an angry response insisting that if Augusta ever does decide to change its policy, it will not be "at the point of a bayonet." The club digs in its heels, rejecting advertising for the 2003 and

2004 tournaments to spare longtime sponsors IBM, Coca-Cola, and Citigroup from potential boycotts and vowing to permanently host the Masters on a commercial-free basis if necessary, but in an effort to avoid stirring up further controversy, Chairman Johnson quietly orders the staff to take down the sign outside the clubhouse that reads NO GIRLZ ALLOUD—THIS MEENS U and issues a confidential request to the members that, for appearances' sake during Masters week, they leave their pet frogs, slingshots, and BB guns in the locker room and refrain from wearing their traditional pirate hats made from folded-up newspapers or jumping out of the azalea bushes in Superman capes improvised from old bedsheets.

Loopy-swinging Jim Furyk scores a convincing and long-overdue victory in a major tournament, winning the U.S. Open at Olympia Fields with a 3-stroke margin and in the process rescuing the USGA from yet another awkward and baffling triumph by an anonymous competitor, in this case little-known Australian runner-up, Stephen Whosis.

Annika Sorenstam, who had just become only the sixth
player ever to complete the career Grand Slam of all four
women's golf major championships, accepts an invitation to play in the Colonial Tournament in Fort Worth.
Although she missed the cut, her barrier-breaking appearance playing with the men, and her participation
later in the year in the Skins Game with Fred Couples,
Phil Mickelson, and Mark O'Meara, set off alarm bells
in the headquarters of the LPGA, whose officials fear
that a potential tsunami of Tiger-whipped, beaten-down,
runner-up male professionals will exploit the new atmosphere of gender equity to enter, and most likely win,
women's competitions. The organization quickly drafts

new Tour regulations requiring that all future entrants in LPGA-sponsored events have clubhead covers with pastel-colored pom-poms hand-knitted by family members or fashioned in the shape of cartoon characters and/or adorable animals; that all players must have a ponytail at least six inches long protruding from the backs of their hats and, weather permitting, must wear shorts and have their legs shaved; and that everyone has to drive a Subaru.

2004

After Phil Mickelson rolls in a 15-foot birdie putt on the 18th hole to clinch the Masters and finally win his first major tournament following so many near misses, he executes an unforgettable leap of pure joy as he seems to visibly shed from his shoulders the burden of years of failed expectations and to almost literally shake the proverbial monkey of unfulfilled promise off his back, and in fact, later that evening, on several separate occasions, members of the Augusta greenkeeping staff reported seeing a left-handed chimpanzee with a sullen, toothy, shit-eating grimace sulking around the club grounds, whimpering audibly and mumbling simian obscenities.

His capacity for dealing with tournament pressures clearly bolstered by head-steadying sessions with gonzo Belgian noodle doctor Jan Vanstiphout, Retief Goosen wins his second U.S. Open as he somehow manages to sink putts on the buzz-cut greens at Shinnecock Hills, which the USGA has inexplicably decided to set up for a game of marbles instead of golf. Following the debacle, Shinnecock's competition committee informs the USGA that after checking the club's schedule of upcoming events, the earliest available date for the course to host another U.S. Open will be in the summer of 2245.

Demonstrating that with their inherently quirky nature, links-style British Open golf courses are as capable of producing an out-of-nowhere champion as the trickiest and silliest setup of a U.S. Open parkland layout, the Claret Jug is won by Todd Whointhehell.

2005

Tiger Woods wins his second British Open with a wire-to-wire victory at St. Andrews, where Jack Nicklaus has fittingly signaled the conclusion of his epochal half-century career in competitive golf with a farewell wave from the bridge over the Swilcan Burn and a parting sink of a tricky par putt on the 18th green. Longtime rival Tom Watson salutes the retirement of his perennial nemesis with a valedictory delivery of fifty pizzas to Jack's suite in the Old Course Hotel, and the Golden Bear responds with a senti- mental middle-of-the-night urgent phone call to Watson asking him if he has Prince Albert in a can.

2006

In time for the start of the season, Augusta National is augmented to 7,445 yards, the par-5 12th at Winged Foot, site of the U.S. Open, will play at 640 yards, and Medinah, where the PGA Tournament will be held, is lengthened to 7,561 yards, which means that efforts to "Tiger-proof" traditional layouts have now proceeded to the point that most championship courses are at least four miles long. The trend toward increased yardages is dictated by the reality that many pros in addition to Woods can now routinely drive the ball a fifth of a mile and are prevented from regularly breaking 60 only by their inability to reliably sink 1/1,000th of a mile putts.

2007

Aging golf prodigy Sergio Garcia misses a heartbreaker of a putt to end up in a tie for the British Open with Padraig

Harrington, who had just staggered off the final hole at Carnoustie after a Van de Velde–worthy two-balls-in-the-burn double bogey. Garcia loses the 4-hole play-off when his ball hits the pin during his replay of the 16th hole and then rockets twenty feet away, costing him a chance at what should have been an easy birdie. In an interview after the defeat, a bitter Garcia blames bad breaks for the outcome, complaining that he feels like he's "playing against a lot of guys out there, more than the field." He's right, of course, but it's not quite as simple as plain old hard luck. In fact, St. Patrick has called in a favor on behalf of the bearer of his saint's name from St. Andrew, and Santiago de Compostella, who would normally have interceded on El Niño's behalf, was busy down in Catalonia, locked in a halo-a-halo supernatural slugfest with St. Jean Baptiste over a World Cup qualifying soccer match between Barcelona and Marseilles, and San Miguel de Allende, who ordinarily would have provided backup, had his stigmata-bearing hands full trying to keep St. Bernard from shepherding Roger Federer to yet another victory over Rafael Nadal in the upcoming Wimbledon Tennis Championship.

Lorena Ochoa wins the first Women's British Open ever held at St. Andrews and overtakes Annika Sorenstam in the world rankings to become the number one player in the world, establishing her as the best Mexican player ever, man or woman, and, considering the dearth of serious competition, making her pretty much of a shoo-in for the outright, overall national title of Best Mexican, period.

2008

Obviously in considerable pain from his injured knee, Tiger Woods turns in a stirring and gutsy performance to outlast a suddenly resurgent Rocco Mediate in a punishing 19-hole Monday play-off to win the U.S. Open at Torrey Pines. Immediately following the awards ceremony, Woods announces that he will take the rest of the season off to undergo reconstructive surgery on his ACL, followed by a period of physical rehabilitation. His statement prompts an immediate and tremendous outpouring of moral support from his fellow players on the Tour, who, faced with the prospect of many months of momentarily winnable Tiger-less tournaments, leave warm personal notes in his locker wishing him an unhurried recovery and send him hundreds of heartfelt get well later cards.

The British Open is won again by that Irish guy—no, not that Irish guy, the other Irish guy, the tall skinny one, not the short stocky one. He also wins the PGA Championship in a little-watched but occasionally thrilling tournament whose Woods-deprived TV coverage is punctuated by countless camera cutaways to shots of the spot in the parking lot where Tiger would have left his car, the position on the driving range where he would have hit warm-up shots, and the section of the practice green where he would have gone through his putting drills.

The U.S. Ryder Cup team under veteran Paul Azinger trounces Nick Faldo's European contingent at Valhalla, scoring the biggest victory margin since 1981 and marking the first time the U.S.A. held the lead after every session of play. Reeling from this mauling at the hands of the Americans, but at the same time bowled over by the sterling performance of controversial captain's pick and noted clotheshorse Ian Poulter, the Europeans decide to hire the flashy dresser's haberdasher to design team uniforms for the 2010 outing that would make a peacock vomit. For its part, the American side is equally impressed by the spectacular play of rookie Boo Weekley and seeks to maintain its dominance of the event by replacing longtime sportswear supplier Ralph Lauren Polo with Weekley's outdoor apparel sponsor, Mossy Oak Camo, and ordering up custom-made horse head motif clubhead covers for the players' drivers so that all team members will be able to ride their big sticks down the fairway cowboy-style in the return match two years hence.

In a move clearly targeted at the young Asian women who now dominate the Tour, and in particular the nearly fifty South Korean golfers, the LPGA announces new conditions of eligibility requiring players who have been on the Tour for two years to demonstrate proficiency in English in an "oral evaluation" or face suspension. Confronted with widespread accusations of racism, the LPGA immediately cancels the policy, deciding that instead of trying to force foreign players to learn English it would probably prove less controversial and more productive in the long run to focus its efforts on getting native players to learn golf.

2009

The United States Court of Appeals for the Federal District confirms its earlier decision that the design of

Titleist's market-dominating Pro V1 golf ball infringes on several patents held by Callaway, and issues an injunction blocking further sales of the product. Titleist responds by announcing that it will replace the previous transgressing model of the overpriced dimpled sphere made from a core of solidified resinous goo and a durable cover of extruded synthetic glop with a new, improved, totally compliant version consisting of an overpriced dimpled sphere composed of a center compounded from solidified viscous goop and an outer impervious layer of molded plastic gunk.

In an effort to rein in the top professionals who are making mincemeat out of even the most demanding courses, the USGA issues new specifications limiting the width and depth of clubface grooves that will take effect in all tournament play immediately following the Masters. The move is intended to prevent skilled professionals from hitting controlled, high-spinning, soft-landing shots out of deep rough, thus restoring the risk of hitting very long drives, which are also often very wild drives. Although the new regulations are aimed primarily at elite, tour-caliber golfers, they will eventually apply to duffers as well, making an already difficult sport that much harder, and the revised rules are said to be only the first of a number of score-wrecking changes contemplated by the lamebrained killjoys of the game's governing body who will ultimately mandate an oval golf ball with little bumps instead of dimples, stipulate that all golf clubs have Medicus-style hinged shafts, and dictate that the spikes on golf shoes be replaced with roller skates.

Dispelling any lingering doubt that he would stage a complete recovery from his knee operation and reclaim his place as the #1 player in the world, Tiger Woods returns to top tournament form with a flourish, in quick succession winning Arnold Palmer's Invitational for the sixth time and Jack Nicklaus's Memorial for the fourth with dramatic finishing rounds to score a decisive pair of postsurgery Tour victories. His trademark come-from-behind charges prompt the recuperated superstar's playing rivals to chip in to buy Woods a passel of thoughtful welcome back gifts, including a series of sky-diving lessons, a full panoply of mountain-climbing gear, a bungee-jumping rig, a tightrope-walking outfit, an inflatable white-water raft, a gas-powered hang glider, a hot-air balloon, a Jet Ski, a speed boat, an all-terrain vehicle, a drag-racing car, a strap-on rocket pack, and a snake-charming set complete with live cobra.

In the golfing gods' most blatant interference with a tournament outcome in the game's long history, the sport's easily peeved divinities right an old wrong by seeing to it that everyone except Angel Cabrera ends up losing the Masters, and the amiable Argentine dons the green jacket that his countryman, personal hero, and friend, Roberto De Vicenzo, was robbed of as the result of a scorekeeping error at Augusta National some four decades earlier. After watching the broadcast of his protégé's stunning victory at his home in Buenos Aires just two days short of his eighty-seventh birthday, De Vicenzo remarks, "What a happy I am," adding, "and what a tacky that jacket is."

Michelle Wie, the temperamental and controversial young female golfing sensation who competed on both the PGA and LPGA Tours and in men's and women's USGA events but has yet to win a single 72-hole tournament, applies for an exemption to play on the senior Champions Tour "with all those guys who never won anything, either." Her application is said to be likely given serious consideration, because although she is three decades shy of her fiftieth birthday, her act is getting very, very, old.

In a sharply worded dissent from the Supreme Court's 5–4 majority decision in *FCC v. Fox Television Stations* upholding penalties for the broadcast of even unscripted and isolated vulgarities previously excused as "fleeting expletives," Justice John Paul Stevens unexpectedly provides a definitive and explicit constitutional defense of the centuries-old tradition of using foul languange on the links when he concludes his argument by noting, "As any golfer who has watched his partner shank a short approach shot knows, it would be absurd to accept the suggestion that the resultant four-letter word uttered on the golf course describes sex or excrement and is therefore indecent."

Living up to its billing as a truly proletarian sporting event, the People's U.S. Open, held for the second time at New York's Bethpage Black public course on Long Island, perfectly captures the spirit of a typical golf outing at a muni: The weather is rotten, the place is a zoo, the rounds take forever, everyone gets plastered, and a

lucky-dork, last-minute entrant nobody has ever heard of cops the trophy and pockets the prize money.

Archaeologists probing the Scottish coast for Viking artifacts stumble on a pit at the edge of the long-abandoned Leith Links that contains several goatskin flasks with traces of a beerlike fermented beverage, a pile of deeply chipped round pebbles, and more than forty shepherds' crooks that appear to have been deliberately broken in half with considerable force. The find is carbon-dated to the year A.D. 1009.